Findings

& FINISHINGS

Findings
& FINISHINGS

Sharon Bateman

A **BEADWORK** HOW-TO BOOK

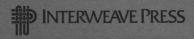
INTERWEAVE PRESS

Illustrations: Ann Swanson, Scott Freeman
Photography: Joe Coca
Cover design: Bren Frisch, Paulette Livers
Interior design: Paulette Livers

Cover images: bottom left, clasp courtesy of Jess Imports; middle right,
necklace courtesy of Cindy Monoghan; others courtesy of the author.
Tables of Contents bottom left, clasp; page 3 carnelian necklace finding; page 22 beetle and hand clasps;
page 25 upper left, leaves courtesy of Burkett Studio. Page 64 toads courtesy of Green Girl Studios.

 INTERWEAVE PRESS

201 East Fourth Street
Loveland, Colorado 80537-5655 USA
www.interweave.com

Printed in Canada by Friesens

Library of Congress Cataloging-in-Publication Data

Bateman, Sharon, 1960-
  Beadwork how-to : findings & finishings / Sharon Bateman.
    p. cm.
  ISBN-13: 978-1-931499-40-8
  ISBN-10: 1-931499-40-3
  1. Beadwork. 2. Jewelry making. 3. Jewelry--Finishing. I. Title.
  TT860.B3337 2003
  745.58'2--dc21
                          2003006316

10 9 8 7 6 5 4

ACKNOWLEDGMENTS

I could not have asked for more positive support than I received from the staff at Interweave Press. Thanks to each of you for all your help, patience, and superb talents. You have done a terrific job and it has been a pleasure working with you.

I also offer a heart-felt thank you to each of the following: Steve Bateman for his loving nature and encouragement, and for coming to the rescue with his computer skills; Petty Officer Christopher Bateman for his casual assumption that I can do everything, his comfortable humor, and serving his country in the United States Navy; Daniel Bateman for his kind spirit and the times he goes out of his way to make my job easier and my life more fun; my mother, Liz White, and my stepmother, Tae Foster, for all their encouragement and love.

A special thanks needs to go to my friends Rebecca Brown-Thompson, Lucy Elle, Jean Campbell, Bill and Cindy Monaghan, Suzanne Golden, Lisa Hobson, Jan Wasser, and Glenda Ulery. Each of you is a blessing and I am incredibly lucky to know you. Glenda, Lucy, Bill, and also Pam Bryson have each contributed their time and talents to help with projects, saving me time for designing.

Contents

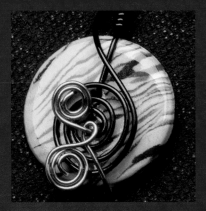

Introduction — 1

Materials and Tools — 7
    Beads — 8
    Threads and Wires — 11
    Tools — 13

Wireworking Basics — 17

Findings — 23
    Head and Eye Pins — 24
    Spacing Bars and Connectors — 27
    Connectors — 30
    Terminals — 34
    Spacers — 43
    Crimps — 44
    Clasps — 46
    Ear Wires — 64
    Pins — 69

Finishings — 71
    Knotting and Anchoring — 72
    Findings with
      Backed Beadwork — 74
    Edgings and Fringes — 76
    Adding Straps to Beadwork — 84

Gallery — 87

Basic Stitches — 107

Suppliers & Resources — 112

Index — 114

INTRODUCTION

Creating jewelry is an awe-inspiring delight! The whole process of making beautiful things transcends both time and experience. Recent technology has given us a range of materials, tools, and finishes, but when you come right down to it, beads still have holes and the clasp is based on a design invented three thousand years ago.

When I hold ancient or vintage jewelry, I often resonate with the artist's sense of achievement in the finished piece and my curiosity is piqued by a sense of mystery—how was this made?

Whether you string or weave beads, I think it's important to remember that skills and techniques passed down by artisans through the centuries provide the foundation for our work today. Acquiring those skills can be difficult, though, and some techniques still seem shrouded in professional secrecy.

That's why I wrote this book: to share trade secrets, to spill the "beads" as it were, and to expand the craft by making accessible one of the more elusive sets of skills—findings and finishings.

Attempting to learn new crafts is often difficult and discouraging. But when you explore skills individually—such as stitching, bending, crimping, tying, and tempering—you gain not only expertise but an enthusiasm that motivates you to learn more. I hope this focused approach helps you advance your skills, emphasize your own sense of style, and lifts even the simplest piece of your jewelry into the realm of art.

Neolithic Beads and Plant Fiber Cord

SNAPSHOTS OF FINDINGS AND FINISHINGS THROUGH HISTORY

Findings have been essential since early humans invented them to pin their clothing together. Materials used for findings and techniques for finishing jewelry have evolved over the years, and here are some highlights.

Jewelry from the Neolithic era—the Stone Age—was made from natural materials. These objects were strung on fibers made from plants or animal sinew. The fibers from that era have long since decayed, but this recent African piece (left) shows a simple tied closure. The loose Neolithic-era beads, left, were likely strung on this type of simple knotted cord.

Sumerian Necklace

The Sumerian necklace (below) is 4,000 years old; the Babylonian bead is from 3,000 years ago.

Sumerians and Babylonians, who ushered in the Bronze Age, incorporated carnelian into their jewelry (right), as well as turquoise and lapis lazuli. They also developed such metalworking skills as casting, forging, soldering metal, and drawing wire. They combined metals into alloys, which makes precious metals durable enough for jewelry.

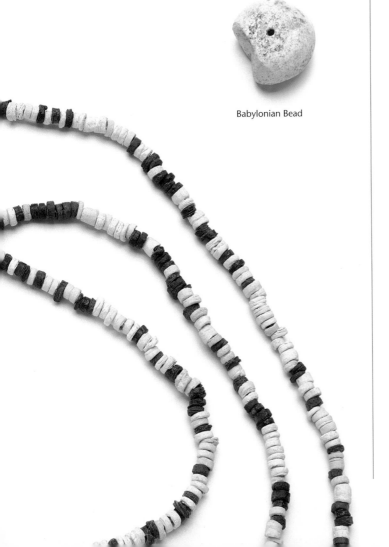

Babylonian Bead

Modern Carnelian necklace

This Roman earring and cloak pin (below) rival the beauty of today's work. Our metalworking techniques may be slightly more refined, but they would still be recognizable to Bronze Age artisans.

Early Egyptians combined metals with other materials to achieve rich color in their work with enamels and glass. Beads were a common element in Egyptian life. Even statues and mummies bore strands of beads. This mummy's necklace (right) has been authenticated to 600 B.C.

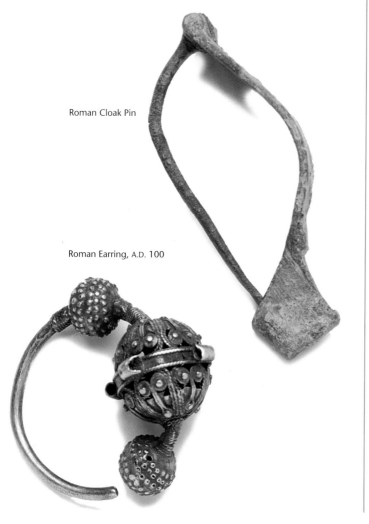

Roman Cloak Pin

Roman Earring, A.D. 100

Mummy Necklace, 600 B.C.

Metal findings, including clasps like these (below), continued to develop over the centuries. Many vintage clasps from the early twentieth century function as fancy centerpieces for necklaces. Clasps were more visible in earlier centuries than they are today—for formal occasions, women chose gowns cut low in the back and wore their hair in upswept styles. In this way, their bare necks became showcases for elaborate clasps.

Vintage Clasps

This traditional Navajo necklace (right) is made of turquoise and silver. The design is similar to ancient Mesopotamian designs, in which the flowers represent pomegranate blossoms and the center pendant represents the new moon.

Navajo Turquoise and Silver Necklace

MATERIALS AND TOOLS

Today, you have a stunning variety of choices when selecting the instruments you will use to create your beading project. Beads, fibers, wire, tools, and other materials are of higher quality and are far more uniform than in the past. Your choice is a matter of personal preference—taking into account the requirements of your project. Included here is an introduction to some of my favorites.

BEADS

Here are just a few of the types of beads you have to choose from when you're creating your unique designs.

SEED BEADS

Seed beads, primarily used for on- and off-loom beadwork, are also beautiful additions between larger beads on a necklace. They come in standard sizes ranging from 15°, which is very small, to 4°, which is about 4mm in diameter. The two most popular seed beads are named for their countries of origin, Japan and the Czech Republic.

Japanese seed beads are shaped like marshmallows, with wide holes that can accommodate coarse thread or many passes of fine thread. Their uniform shape creates a crisp picture when the beads are worked into a flat pattern.

Czech seed beads are shaped like doughnuts and are less uniform than Japanese seed beads. Their round shape gives them a soft look and feel when they're worked into a flat piece. The holes of these beads are smaller than those of Japanese seed beads, which means the bead walls are more durable. However, the holes accept only a few thread passes.

The primary concern in using Czech seed beads is their lack of uniform size. To create a uniform piece with these beads, you must pick out beads as you work, discarding odd-shaped ones. Also, black and other dark colors tend to be smaller than labeled; for example, beads labeled 11° are more often size 12°. However, I think allowing for lack of uniformity and size differences is very much worth the effort, because, in my opinion, Czech seed beads produce the most alluring and satisfying texture of all the seed beads.

Cylinder beads are another type of seed bead. When worked on a loom or into peyote or brick stitch, they create a smooth fabric. The holes in these beads are large enough to take several passes of thread; however, the beads have weak walls. Combining cylinder beads with larger or heavy beads is not a good idea.

The three types of cylinder beads are Delica, Toho, and Magnifica. Delicas and Tohos come in a wider variety of colors, but they are less uniform than Magnificas. Although Magnificas are a little more expensive, I find that they are well worth the cost because they break less often than the other beads. They are also a little smoother around the edges, so they have a softer feel when worked into a bead fabric.

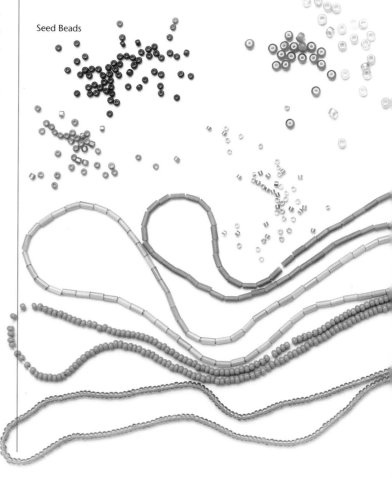

Seed Beads

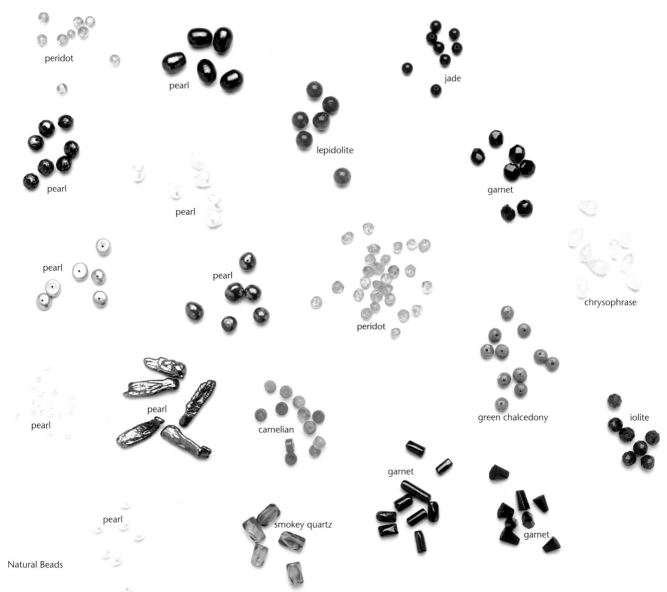

peridot

pearl

jade

lepidolite

pearl

garnet

pearl

pearl

pearl

pearl

peridot

chrysophrase

green chalcedony

iolite

pearl

pearl

carnelian

garnet

garnet

pearl

smokey quartz

garnet

Natural Beads

Bugle beads are long cylinders that come in various lengths; the sides can be round or faceted. The edges of their holes can be sharp and can stress or even cut fine threads; however, they string well on bead wire and are pretty in fringe.

NATURAL BEADS

Stone beads come in many different styles and in a wide variety of types. A few of the most common are druks, nuggets and chips, and faceted beads. Druks are round stones of many sizes. Nuggets and chips have a rougher, more recognizable stone shape; they are usually tumbled to polish them before they are drilled. Faceted stone beads have ground and polished sides to produce sparkle and come in many different shapes.

Freshwater pearls are a nice choice for beading projects. They come in a variety of shapes and are dyed many different colors.

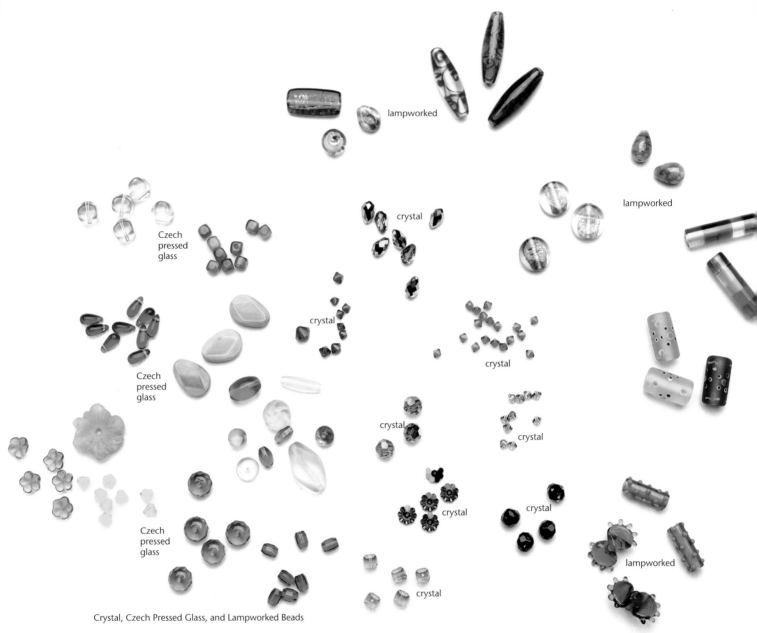

lampworked

lampworked

crystal

Czech pressed glass

crystal

crystal

Czech pressed glass

crystal

crystal

crystal

Czech pressed glass

crystal

crystal

lampworked

crystal

Crystal, Czech Pressed Glass, and Lampworked Beads

GLASS BEADS

Crystals are faceted glass beads, but not all faceted beads are crystal—some faceted beads are pressed glass. You can tell the difference by examining the facets: Crystal has very sharp edges along the facet lines, while a pressed-glass facet has smooth, rounded edges.

Many glass artists produce lampworked beads that are works of art. When choosing a lampworked bead for a piece of jewelry, take into consideration the bead's weight and balance. A beautiful bead does not make up for the discomfort of wearing a piece that weighs you down. Combine a heavy pendant bead with lightweight beads or even fiber that feels good against the skin.

When you're buying beads of any type, be cautious about the finishes. Some colors of beads fade in ultraviolet light; some colors or finishes are lifted off the bead surface by oils in the skin. If you're partway through a piece when you discover that the finish is unstable, you can use an alcohol-based antibacterial lotion to remove the oils from your hands as you complete the piece. When the piece is finished, treat the surface of the beads with spray polyurethane to slow the fading.

THREADS AND WIRES

The biggest consideration in selecting material on which to string beads is strength. Although the best fibers for beadwork are synthetic, silk is also a good option. Also, because it is slick, silk passes easily through beads with small or irregular holes.

However, synthetic fibers have replaced silk because they are easier to work with and less expensive. Many synthetic fibers are more resistant to aging and environmental effects. The most popular synthetic fibers for beading are nylon, polyester, and Kevlar.

Beading wire can be stainless-steel wire treated with a coating, sterling silver, or gold-filled wire.

Nylon-coated beading wire is designed for stringing beads and is flexible enough to use for some simple weaving as well. Always stretch this kind of wire before stringing beads to release kinks. Leave the wire attached to the spool when you're stretching it for a necklace; the spool helps anchor that end of the wire and perhaps saves a few inches. However, do not try to save wire by scrimping; it's better to cut enough to work with than make finishing the piece awkward.

Beading Wire

Braided Beading Cord

Braided beading cord is my preferred stringing material for heavy beads. Even the extra-fine gauge is strong enough for most heavy beads. In spite of its strength, the cord remains supple when it is worked into a piece of jewelry (unless the beads are strung too tight).

Using braided cord takes more skill and preparation than using bead wire. First, you have to prepare the end of the cord for stringing. After you cut it, place a drop of Fray Check on the end and massage it into the fibers to hold them in place and stiffen them so they run through the beads easily.

It is necessary to tie firm knots when you're using this cord. A poorly tied knot dramatically affects the appearance of your piece. Because the cord has no stretch or give, the constant vigilance necessary to keep beads at the right tension is its biggest drawback. If you string beads too tight, they will be so stiff that the piece kinks and has no drape. Overcrowding can wear out or break fragile beads.

ON- AND OFF-LOOM BEADWORK

In bead weaving, you use seed beads and thread to form a beaded fabric. Loomwork requires a loom, frame, or other structure to support your work. One set of threads is strung onto the loom, and beads are tied onto these threads with another set of threads. In off-loom beadwork, a thread secures seed beads in particular stitches. Your finished work can be either flat or three-dimensional.

Only a few types of thread are appropriate for both types of beadwork. Nymo, Silamide, and various braided bead threads are the best for most purposes. Threads such as upholstery threads and Conso are popular, too, but they are more difficult to work with.

Nymo comes in different sizes, colors, and weights. The finest threads are 0 and 00 and are good for the smallest seed beads; B is suitable for large seed beads; D is the most popular size, because it fits a variety of bead sizes. There are slight variances with Nymo. Nymo on a cone feels slightly different than Nymo sold on the bobbin. Colors often impart a different feel to the texture of the thread, too.

Nymo creates a moderately soft, pliable bead fabric that is suitable for most projects. Coating it with beeswax or treating it with Thread Heaven cuts down on the number of knots that may develop. Working with short lengths reduces fraying and wear on the fibers. Unless the finish on your beads is unstable, use a good hand lotion before you work with Nymo—rough skin can shred or weaken fibers.

Silamide is a prewaxed, twisted 2-ply thread. It is thicker than Nymo but can be passed through beads more often with as much ease. It comes in a variety of colors. Bead fabric made with Silamide has a little more body than fabric strung on Nymo. However, Silamide frays if treated roughly. It's more difficult to thread a needle with Silamide than Nymo, but once the needle is threaded it is easy to end or add a new thread.

DandyLine braided bead thread and Bead Smith's Power Pro (the braided bead thread, not the fishing line) are very durable threads that create a supple fabric. They thread and knot as easily as Nymo or Silamide and are not prone to fraying or wear.

Spiderline Fusion (in 10lb/4lb test diameter), a fishing line that has long been overlooked for beading, produces a stiff fabric. Because it does not stretch with tension, it lends itself to three-dimensional work. Although a Kevlar material, it does not cut itself in the work, and using long strands does not make it knot or wear.

TOOLS

NEEDLES

You have many options when you're selecting a needle—different styles are appropriate for different beads and different types of work. For most on- and off-loom beadwork and bead embroidery techniques used

Vintage Needles and Bone Needle Case

in finishing jewelry, a size 12 John James beading needle is appropriate. This type of needle is easy to thread with both Nymo and Silamide and will pass through most beads several times. For projects with beads smaller than 14°, use fine thread and a size 15 needle.

Leather or glover's needles have triangular points for cutting through tough leather.

PLIERS

Round-nose pliers have round, tapered points. Use these pliers to pinch wire and bend it into round shapes, from slight arcs to full looped circles.

Chain-nose pliers have points with a round outside edge and a flat inside edge. The flat edge can come with or without teeth and gives you a firm grip on wire when you're bending it into different positions.

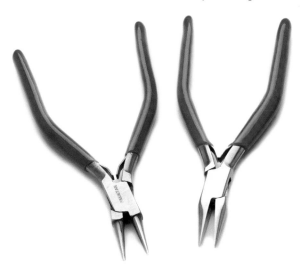

Round-Nose and Chain-Nose Pliers

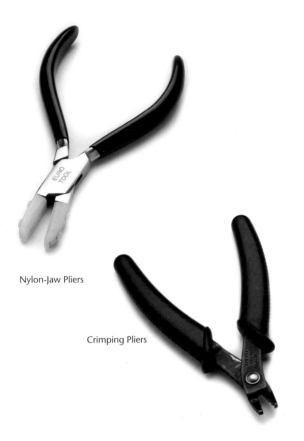

Nylon-Jaw Pliers

Crimping Pliers

EDGE SMOOTHERS

You can use bead reamers to enlarge holes in beads, but they also work well to smooth the inside edges. Bead reamer sets come with an assortment of different-sized tips. Select the tip that's an appropriate size for your bead, insert it into the end of the handle, and screw it into place to secure it. Add a drop of oil onto the tip and push the tip inside the bead's hole. Turn it back and forth to grind away material inside the hole. The oil helps trap the grit.

A cup burr helps you smooth the end of wire. It's a drill bit with a small cup shape on the end whose inside is covered with diamond grit. To smooth the end of wire, insert it in the cup and turn it back and forth repeatedly.

You can also smooth rough ends with a file. Place the file on the metal; push the file forward, then lift it up and pull it back to the starting point before pushing forward across the surface again. Using this back-and-forth movement doesn't harm the metal surface, but it does shorten the life of your file.

Sanding blocks come in many different levels of roughness, called "grit." Move the block back and forth over the end of the wire until it's smooth. Fine

Nylon-jaw pliers consist of a metal frame that holds a set of plastic jaws. These pliers are used primarily for holding wire and straightening it without marring the surface.

Crimping pliers squeeze beads onto wire to secure the ends. For crimping instructions, see page 44.

Crimping Tip of the Millennium

from Lucy Elle

If your crimp bead looks messy no matter how carefully you work the pliers, hold your pliers up to a bright surface and examine the points. They may be rough. Find the high spot on the mouth of the pliers and file it smooth and even.

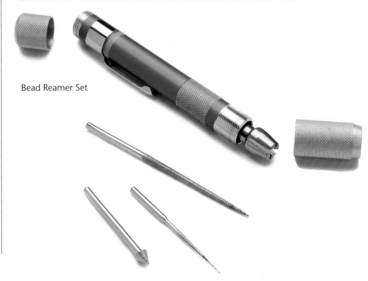

Bead Reamer Set

Sanding Block and Needle File

STARTER STICK

A starter stick is simply a 4-inch-long dowel with holes in it. About 1 inch from one end, drill a hole all the way through the stick with a $\frac{1}{16}$-inch drill bit. About $\frac{1}{4}$ inch from the opposite end, drill two holes perpendicular to each other. With a marker, write the diameter on the end.

You can use this starter stick to serve as a base for a beaded tube or for creating jump rings and for other wireworking projects (see page 17). It can be helpful to have starter sticks in assorted diameters.

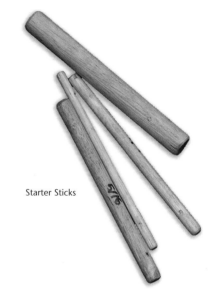

Starter Sticks

grit is best to use with wire. Some blocks are sponges with grit adhered to the surface; they're easier to use than rigid blocks.

HAMMER AND BLOCK

To temper and shape wire, you place the wire on a jeweler's block and pound it with a hammer. Both the hammer and the block should be smooth and clean, with no marks. Placing leather pads under and over the wire as you work will prevent marring the wire surface—very important with color-coated wires.

Pads, Hammer, and Blocks

WIREWORKING BASICS

Some people are intimidated by working with wire—in this case, creating wireworked findings. Wire is far more unforgiving than fiber and, if you make mistakes and discard your project, more expensive. Wire changes as you work with it. Sometimes you want to temper or harden wire; you can actually feel changes in the wire's resistance. Practicing with wire will help you become comfortable, and the best way to start is with inexpensive copper wire from the hardware store. Practice with this wire before you work with sterling silver.

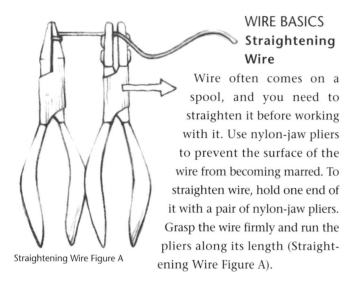

Straightening Wire Figure A

WIRE BASICS
Straightening Wire

Wire often comes on a spool, and you need to straighten it before working with it. Use nylon-jaw pliers to prevent the surface of the wire from becoming marred. To straighten wire, hold one end of it with a pair of nylon-jaw pliers. Grasp the wire firmly and run the pliers along its length (Straightening Wire Figure A).

Measuring Wire

Lay the straightened wire along a ruler to measure it. To mark your measurement, score the wire with an awl or knife or use a permanent pen to draw a line on the wire. Cut the wire with wire cutters.

Cutting Wire

The tips of most wire cutters are angled on one side and flat on the other. Cut wire with the angled side of the cutters facing the length of wire you are cutting off; the flat side of the pliers should face the length of wire you want to use. This technique gives you a flat, smooth end to work with.

Making Pin Points

To use a length of wire as a pin finding, cut the wire at an angle. File the tip into a smooth point.

Bending Wire

When bending wire, use round-nose or flat-nose pliers. Hold the wire firmly with your fingertips and pinch the wire with the tips of the pliers to force the wire over to one side (Bending Wire Figure A).

Making a Loop

Hold the wire firmly with the fingertips. Using the tips of your round-nose pliers, pinch the wire ¼" from the end to force the wire over to one side.

Next move the pliers to the very end of the wire, grasp the end, and roll it up and away from you. As the wire wraps around the curve of the pliers, gently roll the wire over to form a loop (Making a Loop Figure A). You can make larger loops by grasping the wire at a point on the pliers that's closer to the handle.

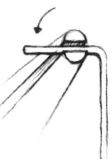

Bending Wire Figure A

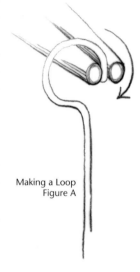

Making a Loop Figure A

Tempering Wire

You can make findings from sterling silver, gold, or craft wire—copper wire coated with colors. Although clasps and pins made of craft wire will not be as strong as other metal findings, at times you will want to use craft wire to match a design or color scheme.

When you're making pins or findings from wire, you want to stiffen (temper) the wire as much as possible to increase its strength. Developing a "feel" for the wire comes in handy when you're tempering, and you develop this feel by practice. Wire hardens as you work it back and forth or pound it—the more you work it, the harder it becomes. Eventually, the wire becomes so hard it is brittle. To learn to recognize that point, try deliberately breaking a few wires by overtempering them. Soon you will sense when the resistance of the wire is hard enough for durability but still not brittle.

To temper the wire of a purchased or existing finding, lay the formed finding on a jewelers' block. Rap the block or chasing hammer firmly on the finding. Test the hardness by gently trying to bend the finding. If the metal is too soft, the finding will bend; if it is too hard, it will break. Repeat the rapping until the finding is as stiff as you desire. If your finding is wire, such as an ear wire, be careful not to hit the finding so hard that you flatten the wire. If you're using a coated wire, cover it with a piece of leather so you do not mar the surface.

When you're working a jump ring or other circular piece, or you're tempering wire in a specific part of a piece, you can gently work the wire back and forth with pliers to harden it.

USING A JIG

A jig can be a handy tool, especially when you want to make identical wireworked pieces like ear wires. Many styles of jigs are available. Each jig is slightly different, so read your jig's instructions before you begin using it.

Keep in mind that anything you do with a jig, you can also do with hand tools, and using a jig isn't a substitute for learning basic wireworking techniques. You still need to know how to measure and temper wire even when you use a jig.

Each jig comes with movable pegs that you set in different patterns in the pegboard for each shape you want to form with wire. Once you've set the pegs, wrap a length of wire around them. Some patterns have a

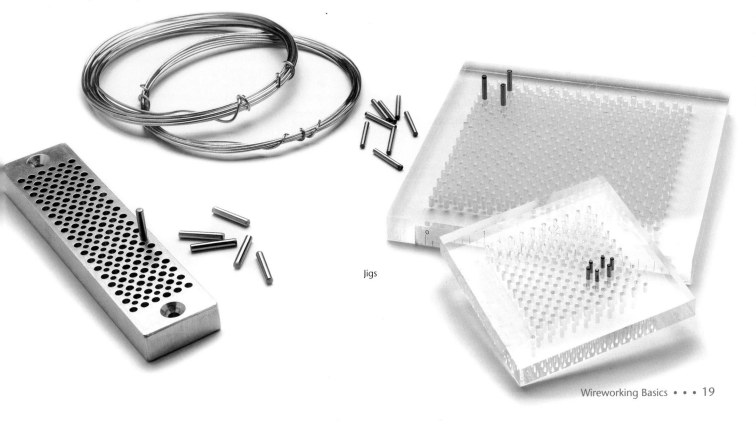

Jigs

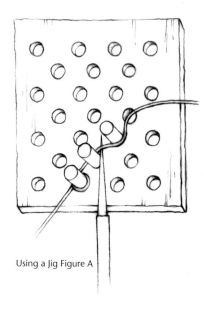

Using a Jig Figure A

starting point and arrows showing where and in what direction to move the wire (Using a Jig Figure A).

Leave a long tail at the beginning of the wrapping so that you have something to tug on to tighten the wire. Using toothed pliers to pull the wire end also helps. The heavier the wire, the more difficult it is to bend around the pegs. Use an awl to push the wire down between the pegs for tight, even loops.

Bead Links

To link components of a piece of jewelry, you can always use jump rings, but you often want something more special. Making a link with beads is a good way to combine the function of the link with the colors and styles of the beads in the piece.

For this technique you need beads and 18- to 24-gauge wire.

Bead Links Figure A

1. Cut a wire 2" long. Slide the beads onto the wire toward the center. Bend up the wire ends in opposite directions (Bead Links Figure A).

2. Trim the wire ends to ½" and smooth them. Creat a loop on one end of the wire (see page 18) (Bead Links Figure B).

Bead Links Figure B

3. Create a second loop on the other end of the bead, so that the loop ends are mirror images.

Connecting Links

You can connect one link directly to another. Use flat- or chain-nose pliers to move the end of the loop sideways, away from the bead. Slide the next link's loop into the opened loop. Bend the loop closed with the pliers (Connecting Links Figure A).

Connecting Links Figure A

Connecting Links with a Jump Ring

You can also connect bead links by inserting jump rings between them. Open a jump ring sideways with the tips of flat-nose pliers. Move the ends away from each other without distorting the shape of the ring. (Connecting Links Figure B). Slide the links onto the ring and close by pushing the ends of the loop back in place.

Connecting Links Figure B

Bead Links

Button Connector Earrings

Button Connector Earrings

Materials

Two 8" lengths of 20-gauge wire
Two 4" lengths of 22-gauge wire
2 buttons
Earring wires

Tools

Wire cutters
Round-nose pliers
Flat-nose pliers

1. Using an 8" length of 20-gauge wire, bend a double loop at one end.
2. Measure the distance from the first hole to the edge of the button and add ¼". Bend the wire at a right angle at that point on the wire.

3. Pass the end of the wire through the hole of the button and bend it up toward the loop. Wrap the wire tightly around the stem. Continue wrapping until the wire covers the stem (Button Connector Earrings Figure A).

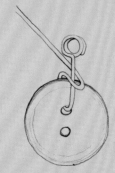

Button Connector Earrings Figure A

4. Bring the end of the wire around to the front of the button. Bend a spiral (see Basic Stitches, page 111) on the end of the wire, bringing the center to rest over the second hole (Button Connector Earrings Figure B).
5. With a 4" length of 22-gauge wire, bend a spiral at one end that measures ¼" across.

Button Connector Earrings Figure B

6. Fold the spiral over and pass the wire down through the first 20-gauge spiral and through the second hole of the button. Bring the wire up and around.
7. Wrap the wire around the first 22-gauge spiral. Bend a loop on the end of the wire and flatten the spiral down over the button (Button Connector Earrings Figure C).
8. Repeat Steps 1 through 7 for the other earring.

Button Connector Earrings Figure C

IDENTIFYING AND USING FINDINGS

Selecting appropriate findings is an important part of the design of your piece. When you're making your selection, keep in mind the role that each finding plays. For example, think of an airport terminal—a place where you transfer from one part of a journey to the next. Similarly, in a piece of beaded jewelry, the terminal is the place where different parts come together. The terminal of your work is like the end of a flight. A connector is like the walkway that links you to the next part of the journey. A clasp is the final stage of the journey, like going home.

Even though the terminal, connectors, and clasp can be completely different from one project to the next, they all serve the same purpose and work in essentially the same ways from piece to piece. A well-designed piece has a smooth transition from the beadwork to the parts that complete it, make it functional, and give it purpose. The transition from the body of your beadwork—the terminal—needs to be neat, secure, and logical. The connectors and clasp do not need to be invisible, but they should not be in jarring contrast to the beadwork.

Findings serve many different purposes in finished pieces of jewelry. In this chapter, we consider the following components.

- *Head and eye pins*—used to thread beads on for dangles and earrings
- *Spacers and spacing caps*—serve to visually separate components in a piece of jewelry
- *Spacing bars and spacing connectors*—let you create multi-strand pieces of jewelry
- *Connectors*—join or connect individual components of a piece
- *Terminals*—prepare the ends of a piece of beadwork for the transition from the beadwork to the clasp
- *Crimps*—help secure the ends of beadwork
- *Clasps*—hold together the two ends of a finished piece, such as a bracelet or necklace
- *Earring wires and pins*—attach to your beadwork for wearing

Some of these findings are essentially the same thing in different shapes. We call each type of finding by its most common name, but even if you find it called something different, it works in the same fashion.

HEAD AND EYE PINS

A head pin is a wire with a nail-like head on one end. The head holds the beads on the wire. The other end of the pin is made into a loop. You can attach head pins to ear wires, necklaces, or other types of connectors or clasps with the loop.

Some manufactured head pins can be quite pretty, with differently shaped heads. Pins with flat heads are called paddles. Pins with a loop at the end are called eye pins.

Although manufactured pins are inexpensive and convenient to use, at times you will want a different

Head Pins

length or finish. Making your own head pins is easy and adds a special touch to a project.

Eye Pins

To make an eye pin, simply bend a loop on the end of a short piece of wire (Eye Pin Figure A). The wire should be at least 1" longer than you want for the finished piece.

Eye Pin Figure A

Staple Bend Pins

In this version of a head pin, a tight bend at the bottom of a wire serves as the head.

1. With a 3" or 4" length of wire, use chain- or flat-nose pliers to bend a curve at one end.

Staple Bend Pin Figure A

Staple Bend Pin Figure B

Staple Bend Pins

2. Pinch the curve tightly closed (Staple Bend Pin Figure A).

3. Cut off the end of the wire, being careful not to cut the pin. Place beads on the wire. Bend a regular loop (see page 18) on the other end of the wire (Staple Bend Pin Figure B).

Basic Earrings

USING HEAD PINS

Head pins are an easy way to add components to many projects. Slight variations in your head pins, both manufactured and the ones you create yourself, can add a little extra style to your piece. The tips and techniques offered here are just a few of the many applications for this useful component.

Basic Earrings, 2

Basic Earrings, Part 1

For this technique, you need head pins, beads, and ear wires.

1. Add beads and findings to a head pin. Bend a loop at the top.

2. Connect directly to the ear wire by opening the ear-wire loop, sliding the wrapped loop on, and closing it.

Basic Earrings, Part 2

For this technique, you need eye pins, beads, and ear wires.

1. Add beads and findings to an eye pin. Bend a loop at the top.

2. Connect directly to the ear wire by opening the loop on the ear wire, adding the eye-pin loop, and closing the ear wire loop. Add a bead link (see page 20), if desired. Open the loop of the bead link sideways and add it to the bottom loop of the eye pin. Then open the ear-wire loop sideways and connect it to the top loop of the eye pin.

Squiggle Pins

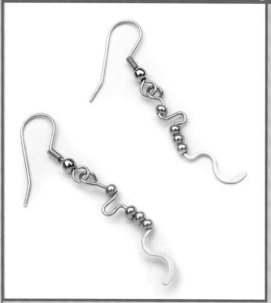

Squiggle Pins

When you're selecting the wire for this project, be sure to use wire that isn't filled. The inside metal of a filled wire will show in the finished pins. For example, if you use gold or silver filled wire, the copper shows through. The silver or gold coating is so thin that the surface wears off while you are working, and the slightest nick reveals the different colored metal underneath the surface.

Materials
2" to 4" of 20- or 18-gauge wire

An assortment of beads as desired

Tools
Anvil or steel block

Chasing hammer

Wire cutters

Round-nose pliers

Extra fine sanding block

Masking tape

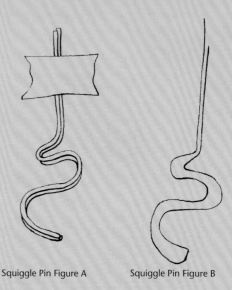

Squiggle Pin Figure A   Squiggle Pin Figure B

1. Cut two equal lengths of wire. Lay them side by side. Tape the two wires together (Squiggle Pin Figure A).
2. Use round-nose pliers to bend both wires into a pleasing shape. Remove tape.
3. Pound the wire ends, starting at the end of the squiggle design and working down, so that the whole tip is tapered flat. Use the sanding block to smooth and shape each tip (Squiggle Pin Figure B).

To use these pins with a single bead, slide the bead on and bend a loop at the top (Squiggle Pin Figure C).

Squiggle Pin Figure C

Head Pin Ear Wires

Design courtesy of Lisa Hobson

You can create ear wires from head pins instead of using separate ear-wire findings. Be sure to use tempered sterling silver, not base metal, pins.

1. Bend a closed loop at the head end of the head pin.
2. Form the other end of the head pin into a curve around a starter stick.
3. Add beads to another head pin and attach to the ear wire with a loop (Head Pin Wires Figure A).

Lisa Hobson's Head Pin Ear Wires

Seed Bead Spirals

Design courtesy of Lisa Hobson

Add seed beads to a head pin and bend a loop at the top. Wrap the beaded pins around a starter stick in a spiral pattern. Use the loop at the top to hang on ear wires.

Head Pin Wires Figure A

Seed Bead Spirals

Bead-Stacked Pins

Head pins do not always need to be straight. When you're using a flat bead, it is often appealing to bend the head of the pin so the head is to the back (Stacked Ear Wires Figure A). Experiment with bending the wire stem up or arcing it to the back to achieve the proper balance.

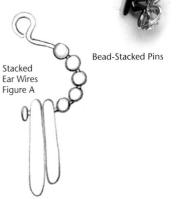

Stacked Ear Wires Figure A

Bead-Stacked Pins

SPACING BARS AND SPACING CONNECTORS

Spacing bars come in many styles. They can be simple or fancy, but are generally strips with holes. Spacing bars separate the strands of a multistrand piece of jewelry—a necklace or bracelet, for example—to better control their position. Keep in mind that to make the strands of a multistrand necklace lie properly, you need to make the outside strands slightly longer than the inside strands.

Spacing connectors use rings to separate strands. With a spacing connector, you can create a multistrand necklace and still use a single-strand clasp.

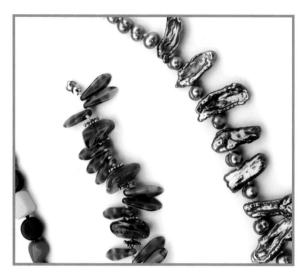

Knotted Cord Spacing

Knotted Cord Spacing

Another way to space beads is to form knots with the thread or cord. (See instructions, page 72, for knot-tying steps.) For this technique, you need beads and cord.

1. Use 3 times as much cord as you want in the finished length. Attach one end to the clasp or terminal to be used, usually a bead tip.
2. String a bead; tie a multiple overhand knot around the tip of an awl. Use the awl to slide the knot up close to the bead. Tighten the knot as you slide out the awl tip (Knotted Cord Figure A).
3. Repeat between each bead.

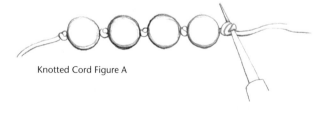

Knotted Cord Figure A

BEAD CAPS

Bead caps give a finished look and just a little extra style to your work. They sit over the bead's hole and can be slightly concave, resting delicately over the bead, or they can be created with seed beads. You slide bead caps onto the wire or cord so that the bowl shape is facing the hole of the bead.

Use these bead caps on a head pin for earrings, or combine them with an Omega Terminal or Teddy Bear Terminal and incorporate them into a piece of jewelry. Place these caps next to beads that have a large diameter.

These bead caps will have a different surface texture, depending on the stitch you use. Either gives a little extra flourish. It is a nice way to add some extra interest to simple earrings, add some color to your terminal, or make a simple foundation for seed bead tubes.

Seed Bead Cap

This bead cap is easy to create with seed beads, beading thread, and a needle. For square-stitch instructions, see page 111.

1. String 5 beads; pass through all again to form a circle.

Bead Caps

2. Square-stitch 2 beads onto each of the 5 beads. Pass through the first set to close the round.

3. Square-stitch 2 beads onto each of the 10 beads. Pass through the first set to close the round (Bead Cap Figure A).

4. This round is optional. Stitch 2 beads onto 2 beads all around. Pass through all again to tighten up.

5. Work as many rounds as you wish. Working bead-for-bead will extend the length only; increasing the square stitch will enlarge the tube (Bead Cap Figure B).

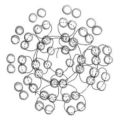

Bead Cap Figure A   Bead Cap Figure B

Square-Stitched Seed Bead Cap

For this cap, you will need seed beads, beading thread, and a beading needle.

Square-Stitched Bead Caps

Round 1: String 4 beads and tie them into a circle.

Round 2: Square-stitch 2 beads onto each of the beads. Pass through the first set to close the round.

Round 3: Square-stitch 2 beads onto each of the beads. Pass through the first set to close the round.

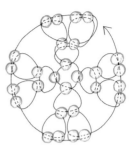

Square-Stitched Bead Cap Figure A

Round 4 and after: These rounds are optional. Square-stitch bead for bead for 1 or more rounds (Square-Stitched Bead Cap Figure A). Finish when you reach your desired width.

Peyote-Stitched Seed Bead Cap

For this cap, you will need seed beads, beading thread, and a beading needle.

Peyote-Stitched Bead Cap

Round 1: String 4 beads and tie into a circle.

Round 2: String 1 bead and pass through the next bead of the last round. Continue around the circle. Pass through the first bead to close the round.

Round 3: String 2 beads and pass through the next bead of the last round. Continue around. Pass through the first 2 beads to close the round.

Round 4: String 1 bead and pass through the next bead of the last round. Continue around. Pass through the first bead to close the round (Peyote-Stitched Bead Cap Figure A).

Rounds 5 and after: These rounds are optional. String 1 bead and pass through the next bead of the last round. Continue around. Pass through the first bead to close the round.

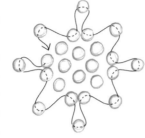

Peyote-Stitched Bead Cap Figure A

Working with Seed Bead Tubes

When you're making a tube that is difficult to work off the 4-bead center, you can work peyote- or square-stitched bead caps and use them as bases for your tube. It is easier to make both bead caps at once than to stop to make a second one at the end of your project.

1. Make a bead cap and increase on each round until you have the number of beads needed to work your tube. Secure your thread.
2. Make a second cap. Make an Omega Terminal (see page 38) or Teddy Bear Terminal (see page 39) on each bead cap.
3. Work the tube off of the edge of the bead cap.
4. Sew the second bead cap onto the tube. Secure your thread.

CONNECTORS

JUMP RINGS

Jump rings connect one object to another. They are easy to make (see page 30), but it is often simpler to use manufactured ones when the color of the metal in your piece matches the metal rings.

Using a Jump Ring

1. Open a jump ring with the tips of a flat-nose pliers, moving the ends sideways so you don't distort the ring's circular shape.
2. Slide the links of the piece onto the ring.
3. Close the jump ring by pushing the ends of the loop sideways until they are back in place.

MAKING CONNECTORS

Knowing how to make your own connectors gives you an easy alternative to using manufactured connectors. With a little practice, you will find they are no trouble at all to incorporate into your designs.

Making Jump Rings

Manufactured jump rings are easy to use and inexpensive; however, if you need a certain color to match a wire project or if you need a jump ring you don't have at home, you can make your own with wire wrapped over a starter stick.

1. Run the end of a length of wire through a hole on one end of the starter stick (see page 15) that is the diameter of the desired jump ring. The tail sticking up can serve as a handle.
2. Firmly hold the wire against the starter stick. Turn the dowel with your other hand, letting the wire slide through your hands and wrap around the stick. Lay each ring beside the previous one as you turn the dowel.
3. Once you have a number of rings wrapped around the starter stick, clip the wire running through the hole. Slide the coil off the starter stick. Use the cutters to cut off each ring. Cut flat and perpendicular to the wire or at opposite angles so the points fit together flush.
4. File each end flat and smooth with a needle file if needed.

Bails with Pendants

Square-Stitched Beaded Bail

BAILS

Bails, a specific part of most findings, are the rings or loops that attach one thing to another. A clasp may have a bail. A pendant has a loop that forms the bail. The bail part of a terminal attaches the piece to the closure or the place where you suspend a pendant or bead.

Square-Stitched Beaded Bail

For this technique, use a small assortment of seed beads that complement a strand necklace and pendant you plan to use. You also need a beading needle and thread (Silamide or Nymo) appropriate for the size of seed beads you're using.

The beaded bail is worked separately from the strand necklace. You slide it over the strand.

For square stitch instructions, see page 111.

1. Thread the needle with a comfortable length of beading thread. String enough seed beads to wrap around the beads of the strand. Skipping the last bead strung, pass back through all of the beads. Pass through from the opposite direction in which you tied on to the strand (Beaded Bail Figure A).

Beaded Bail Figure A

2. String 3 beads. Square-stitch (see Basic Stitches, page 111) them to the end bead of the previous row. String 3 beads and work the last 2 beads onto the next 2 beads of the previous row. Square-stitch two beads at a time up to the end bead on the opposite end. String 4 beads and work the last 3 beads onto this point bead.

3. String 3 beads and square-stitch them to the point bead of the previous row. Square-stitch two beads at a time up to the first beads of the row. String 1 bead and pass through the first two beads (Beaded Bail Figure B).

point bead

point bead

Beaded Bail Figure B

4. Work the rows until you have the width and look you want for the bail. End by double-stitching the last point set and exiting from the point bead.

5. String enough beads to accommodate the pendant or bead. Pass through the opposite point bead and back through the beads just added. Repeat to strengthen the beads and fill the holes. Secure the thread.

Wire Bails and Clasps for Beadwork with Backing

To make a wire bail for beadwork that has a backing, follow these steps.

1. Cut a length of 20-gauge wire 1½" wider than the piece to be bailed. Bend a loop at each end. Squiggle the wire through the center.

2. Scuff the wire with a coarse sanding block and clean the wire with fingernail polish remover.

3. Place a small amount of epoxy on the backing. Lay the scuffed wire on the backing, placing the loops at the edges. Place the beadwork on top of it. Allow the glue to set following manufacturer's directions (Wire Bail, Backed Beadwork Figure A).

Wire Bail, Backed Beadwork Figure A

Use wire or links connected to the bails to attach the backed beadwork to a strap or another component.

For earrings or pendants that hang from the top, form a looped bobby-pin shape (Wire Bail, Backed Beadwork Figure B).

To make wire clasps for backed beadwork, follow these steps.

Wire Bail, Backed Beadwork Figure B

1. Cut two 18- or 20-gauge wires 3 times longer than the pieces. Bend one in half and the second with a round open end. Bend loops at each end, making sure that they are positioned in an appropriate place for the beadwork (Wire Bail, Backed Beadwork Figure C).

Wire Bails for Backed Beadwork

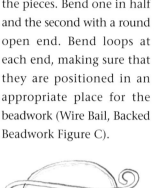

Wire Bail, Backed Beadwork Figure C

2. With epoxy, glue the beadwork to the backing, sandwiching the clasp halves in between.

3. Bend the hook for the clasp (Wire Bail, Backed Beadwork Figure D).

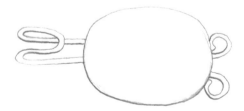

Wire Bail, Backed Beadwork Figure D

Monkey's Fist Pendant Bail

Monkey's Fist Pendant Bail

Materials
4½" of 18-gauge wire
Leather cord
Flat pendant with hole
   facing the front

Tools
Wire cutters
Round-nose pliers
Chain-nose pliers
Ruler

Monkey's Fist Bail Figure C   Monkey's Fist Bail Figure D

1. Using chain-nose pliers, bend one end of the wire 1½" from the end. Slide the pendant onto the long end of the wire.
2. Bend the long end up and over the pendant. Bend over the short end on the right-hand side of the long wire (Monkey's Fist Bail Figure A).
3. Bend the short wire up, parallel to the pendant (Monkey's Fist Bail Figure B).
4. Begin wrapping the long end around the short end. Wrap 3 times, ending with the wire to the left of the short end when the pendant is facing front (Monkey's Fist Bail Figure C).

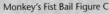

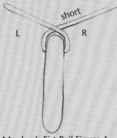

Monkey's Fist Bail Figure A

Monkey's Fist Bail Figure B

5. Using the round-nose pliers, bend a loop with the short wire just above the 3 wraps (Monkey's Fist Bail Figure D).
6. Arc the short wire into a second loop and tuck the end up under the 3 wraps (Monkey's Fist Bail Figure E). Arc the long wire slightly up and then around the two top loops. Loop the end around and tuck it inside the top loops just above the 3 wraps (Monkey's Fist Bail Figure F).
6. Pass a cord through the two top loops. You can also use a jump ring to attach it to a second bail or terminal.

Monkey's Fist Bail Figure E

Monkey's Fist Bail Figure F

Making a Wire Bail

Materials

One 12" to 24" length of 18-gauge wire

³⁄₁₆" starter stick

Bent-Wire Bail

1. Cut and straighten the wire. Run one end through a hole on the starter stick. Using the tail of wire to help hold the stick firmly, turn the stick and begin winding the wire on. Work 3 or more turns (Wire Bail Figure A).

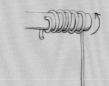

Wire Bail Figure A

2. Using round-nose pliers, bend a small loop up close to the wound wire.

3. Wind an equal amount of wire, turning the starter stick in the opposite direction (Wire Bail Figure B). Cut the wire above the hole and remove the wire tail. Trim the ends evenly. Pass a cord through the bail and add a terminal. Use a jump ring or other connector to attach a pendant.

Wire Bail Figure B

TERMINALS

Sometimes terminals are incorporated into the design of the clasp. However, sometimes they are separate techniques that you use to finish the end of your strap and prepare it to be attached to a clasp.

Terminals should be secure and durable without being hazardous to the wearer. Necklaces need terminals or clasps that give or break away when tugged hard so they won't hurt the wearer if they accidentally catch on something.

MANUFACTURED TERMINALS

A variety of terminals are manufactured for the jewelry designer. They are simple to use, with the right tools, and each adds a nice touch to your projects. It takes a little experience to develop suitable terminals for specific projects. It may also be worthwhile to practice using the terminals a few times before you add them to a special piece.

Spring Terminals

A spring terminal is a sturdy spring in which the last loop forms the bond with the strap. Use these terminals with leather cord or rattail (fiber cord with a satin finish). Spring terminals give you an excellent way to make a quick and casual necklace that showcases a special bead.

With flat-nose pliers, gently close or bend the last coil of the spring to clamp the spring onto the cord and hold it in place. When you're using rattail or other cords that fray easily, first treat the end with Fray Check or G-S Hypo Cement before clamping the spring onto the cord.

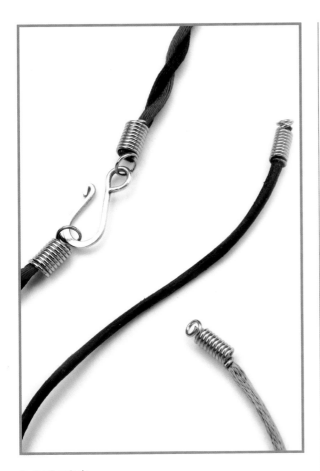

Spring Terminals

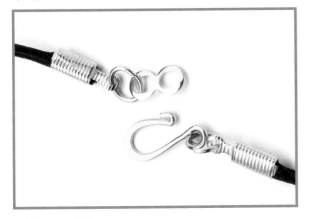

Fold-Over Terminals

Fold-Over Terminals

A fold-over terminal is like a crimp bead, but it is applied in a different way. The "flaps" are folded over the end of a cord to pinch it in place and give you a neat end ready for a clasp.

Place the end of the cord inside the fold-over terminal. Using flat-nose pliers, pinch one side closed. Repeat on the other side. Attach to a clasp with jump rings or connectors.

Wired Bullet Ends

Bullet ends are like a collar or cap that neatly cover knots or other terminals.

Wired Bullet Ends

Tie the ends of the strands in a loose knot, close to the beads. Slide the end of a length of wire through the center of the knot. Add Fray Check to the center of the knot. Tighten the knot around the wire. Using

Wired Bullet Ends Figure A

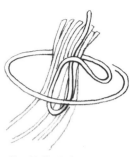

Glued Bullet Ends Figure A

round-nose pliers, bring the end of the wire up and wrap around the stem of the wire (Wired Bullet Ends Figure A).

To use bullet ends with crocheted tubes, tie the thread tail onto a loop of wire. Run the opposite end of the wire up through a bullet or cone end. Use round-nose pliers to form a loop or a wrapped loop on the top end of the bullet cap. Trim and attach to a clasp or link.

Glued Bullet Ends/Bolo Terminals

Glued bullet ends are glued onto the terminal of a tube or strand bracelet, necklace, or bolo tie. They are like a metal cap that gives your work a more professional look; they also have a ring that you can attach

to a clasp. For this technique you need binding cord and jeweler's glue, in addition to your strand and ends.

1. Prepare the ends of the strands. With a binding cord, form a loop and lay it against the ends of the strands. Wrap the binding cord tightly around the end, beginning opposite to the loop and working toward it (Glued Bullet Ends Figure A).

2. Once you reach the loop, run the end of the cord through it. Tug the end of the loop to pull the loop up under the binding (Glued Bullet Ends Figure B).

3. Trim the ends of the strands even at about ¼" from the binding. Fill the bullet end about half-full of glue. Holding it upright, push the end of the strands down into it (Glued Bullet Ends Figure C). Wipe away any excess glue. Let dry thoroughly, according to manufacturer's directions.

Glue bolo tips in the same way. To add a dangle or pendant on the tips, add a spring terminal.

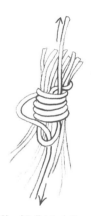

Glued Bullet Ends Figure B

Glued Bullet Ends

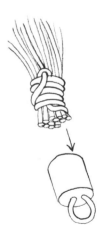

Glued Bullet Ends Figure C

Bead Tips and Clamshell Bead Tips

A bead tip is a small, basket-shaped component that cradles the knot on the end of a strand made with cord or thread. It provides a ring where you can attach the clasp. Tips give terminals a subtle finish, one that is not as noticeable as other findings.

Bead Tips

Clamshell Bead Tips

With the cord coming off the spool, string the desired number of beads and a bead tip, with the loop facing toward the end. Tie a multiple overhand knot on the end of the cord (see page 72 for knot-tying techniques). Make sure that the knot will not pull

through the bead tip (Bead Tip Figure A).

Slide the beads down toward the end of the knotted cord. Hold the strand up so that the weight of the beads holds it straight down. Cut the cord 6–8" from the last bead. Add a second bead tip facing away from the beads. Use tweezers or knot pliers to tie a knot inside the second bead tip.

Trim both tails and add a drop of glue or Fray Check to each knot. Use round-nose pliers to bend the loops on the tips over into place.

The clamshell bead tip is decorative in that the closed halves resemble a bead. Use the clamshell tip if you do not want the thread to be seen, even on close inspection.

Work clamshell bead tips in the same way as a bead tip (Clamshell Tip Figure A). After the knots are secure, carefully close the shell with flat-nose pliers (Clamshell Tip Figure B).

Please note: Using bead tips takes practice! The first knot is very easy, because the tip slides down the cord to meet it. The second knot is difficult. A kink in your beads or the slightest slip of your knotting tools will leave a gap between the tip and the beads on the finished piece. Before you let go with the knotting tool, double-check the spacing of the beads. For specific knotting instructions, see page 72.

Bead Tip Figure A

Clamshell Tip Figure A

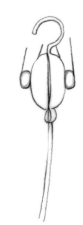

Clamshell Tip Figure B

TERMINALS TO MAKE

You can create terminals for your jewelry in many different ways. Knowing how to create your own terminals is helpful for those times when the variety of manufactured ones do not complement your work.

Two-Hole Bead Terminal

Spacer or Two-hole Terminal

For this technique, you need two 8mm beads with two holes and flat backs, and some 20-gauge wire.

1. Cut 2" of wire. Bend a double loop in the center. Trim the wire ends to a length that is 1½ times the width of the two-hole bead (Two-Hole Terminal Figure A).

2. With a flat-nose pliers, bend the ends of the wires toward each other (Two-Hole Terminal Figure B). Set the ends of the wire on either side of the bead so they are just inside the first hole.

Two-Hole Terminal Figure A   Two-Hole Terminal Figure B

3. Put one point of the round-nose pliers into the loop and push into the wire with the other point. The wire will arc and tighten the points of the terminal into the holes (Two-Hole Terminal Figure C).

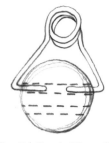

Two-Hole Terminal Figure C

SEED BEAD TERMINALS

Seed bead terminals take a few more minutes to create than many of the other terminals, but the extra time is worth the detail and style these terminals give your jewelry. Here are two I've developed.

Omega Terminal

This style of wire connector is designed to be used with the African Helix, the Inverted African Helix, or any seed-bead project that forms a hollow tube. It simplifies adding a clasp and also reduces wear on the threads.

For this terminal, use two 4" wires, two 6mm or 8mm beads that match the beads for the project, two 4mm beads, and round-nose pliers. In addition, you need seed beads and thread for the beadwork itself.

1. Using round-nose pliers, bend a double loop at one end of a 4" wire. Slide one of the 4mm beads onto the wire. Repeat on the second wire.

2. Work your seed bead project around the Omega Terminal wire. (See stitches, page 108, for helix, peyote stitch, and netting.)

Omega Terminal
Figure A

3. To finish the terminal, add the 6mm or 8mm bead to the wire and form a loop on the end with round-nose pliers.

Teddy Bear Terminal

The Teddy Bear Terminal has a soft, more flexible feel than the Omega Terminal does. It also gives you a chance to use a clasp made with seed beads and a special button or bead that may suit a beaded tube. For this terminal, you need seed beads, a large connector bead that will not show, a large clasp bead that will be part of the clasp, beading thread, and a beading needle.

1. Pass through 1 seed bead twice to make a stop bead. String a larger bead (the connector bead), spacer seed beads, the clasp bead, and 1 more seed bead that will serve as the second stop bead. Skipping the last seed bead, pass through all beads just strung. Pass through all again twice (if possible) to strengthen. Secure the thread (Teddy Bear Terminal Figure A).

2. For the second half of the clasp, repeat Step 1, but replace the clasp bead with a loop just large enough to go around the clasp bead (Teddy Bear Terminal Figure B).

Teddy Bear Terminal Figure A

Teddy Bear Terminal Figure B

To attach the Teddy Bear Terminal, push the connector bead down into a tube of beadwork and stitch the tube closed around and over the bead.

Seed Bead Terminals with Peyote Stitch

For this technique you will need seed beads, beading thread, and a beading needle for the peyote-stitched tube.

Seed Bead Terminals with Peyote Stitch

Work one end of two Omega or Teddy Bear Terminals. If you use a Teddy Bear Terminal, finish the terminal completely and work the tube around the stop bead inside the tube. If you use an Omega Terminal, use the wire as a handle for beginning the tube. Once the tube is well started, finish making the terminal.

Beginning

1. String 4 beads. Pass through all to form a circle and tie a knot (Terminal with Peyote Figure A). String 1 bead and pass through the next bead of the circle. Repeat all around. Pass through the first bead of this round. Add the terminal at any time to help hold the piece as you work.

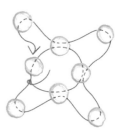

Terminal with Peyote Figure A

2. String 2 beads. Pass through the next bead of the last round. Repeat all around. Pass through the very first bead of this round (Terminal with Peyote Figure B).

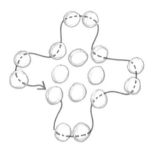

Terminal with Peyote Figure B

3. String 1 bead. Pass through the second bead of the 2-bead set of the last round. String on 1 bead. Pass through the first bead of the 2-bead set of the last round. String on 1 bead. Pass through the second bead of the 2-bead set of the last round. Repeat all around. Pass through the first bead of this round (Terminal with Peyote Figure C).

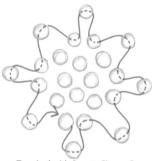

Terminal with Peyote Figure C

Repeat Steps 2 and 3 until you have the diameter you want for your tube. At this point, finish the Omega Terminal so it will not slide down inside the tube as you work. If you are using the Teddy Bear Terminal to start your work, you can work the loop or bead at this stage.

Ending

1. Decrease on the rounds of the peyote tube until you have 4-bead rounds. Pass your thread through all 4 beads.

2. Slide the Omega Terminal or Teddy Bear Terminal down into the center. Pull the thread tight and secure. Work the outside half of either connector here.

Seed Bead Terminals with Netting

Seed Bead Terminals with Netting

Work one end of two Omega or Teddy Bear Terminals. In addition, you will need seed beads, beading thread, and a beading needle for the netted tube.

1. String 4 beads. Pass through all to form a circle and tie a knot.

2. String an odd number of beads and pass through the next bead of the circle. Repeat all around. Pass through the first beads of this round and through the center bead in the set. You can add the terminal at any time to help hold the piece as you work (Terminal with Netting Figure A).

3. Work the netting for the desired length. To end, pass through the odd beads of the last round. Slide the second Omega Terminal or Teddy Bear Terminal into the center. Pull the thread tight and secure.

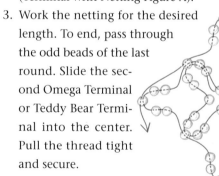

Terminal with Netting Figure A

Love Knots

A love knot is a sliding knot that attaches the ends of a leather cord so that the length is adjustable.

Materials

36" of 2mm leather cord
Pendant bead and accent beads that cord fits through

Love Knots

1. String a pendant bead and the accent beads and center them on the cord.
2. Lay out one end; it will be the anchor cord for the first knot. Bring the opposite end over and under the anchor cord [a] and then over itself [b], to form a loop. Bring the end through the loop [c]. The anchor cord should lie inside the loop but not be involved in tying the knot (Love Knot Figure A).

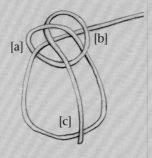

Love Knot Figure A

3. Tighten the knot by arranging the loop until it cinches up around the anchor cord.
4. Repeat the process with the other end, this time using the anchor cord to tie your knot. Trim the tail close.

Eyeglass Terminals

These terminals are a dominant feature, so they need to be as attractive as possible.

Materials

24" to 42" of 49-strand nylon-coated beading wire
2 crimp beads
Seed beads to cover the eyeglass terminal loops
Beads for 18" to 36" for the strap
2 eyeglass terminals

Eyeglass Terminals

Tools

Crimping pliers
Wire cutters

1. String the crimp bead and enough seed beads to make a loop. Pass the beads through the loop of the eyeglass terminal. Pass the end of the bead wire through the crimp bead and squeeze it. (For crimping instructions, see page 44.)
2. String 18" to 36" of beads. Work a second loop of seed beads around the loop of the eyeglass terminal (Eyeglass Terminal Figure A).

Eyeglass Terminal Figure A

Omega Connector with
Jump Ring Terminal

Crochet Ropes and Jump Ring Terminals

For this technique, you'll need enough crochet thread and beads for the desired project, 2 jump rings, and materials for either Omega or Teddy Bear Terminals.

1. Slip-stitch thread onto the crochet hook. Run the hook through the center of the jump ring and hook it onto the thread.
2. Pull the thread through and single crochet 1 stitch over the ring. Single crochet 16 stitches onto the jump ring. Slip-stitch to close the round. Leave a 6- or 8-inch tail (Crocheted Rope with Jump Ring Figure A).

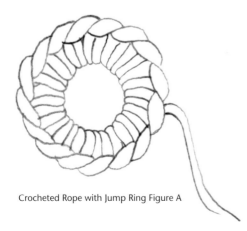

Crocheted Rope with Jump Ring Figure A

3. Repeat Steps 1 and 2 to make a second ring, but do not cut the thread at the end.
4. Begin crocheting with the beads. Work a few rounds. Once you have a good start, create a Teddy Bear or Omega Terminal through the jump ring. (Crocheted Rope with Jump Ring Figure B).

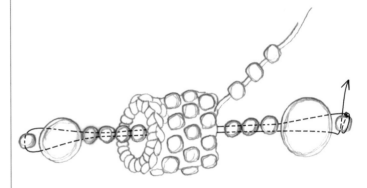

Crocheted Rope with Jump Ring Figure B

5. Continue crocheting to the length desired. Slip-stitch to close the round and trim the thread
6. Make a Teddy Bear Terminal on the second ring. Use the tail of thread to sew the second half of the terminal on the end of your crochet tube (Crocheted Rope with Jump Ring Figure C).

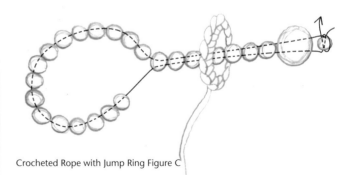

Crocheted Rope with Jump Ring Figure C

SPACERS

Spacers are used for many reasons. They protect fragile beads from rubbing and wearing down. They also add a subtle elegance or a more finished look while reducing the number of expensive beads needed to complete a piece.

Spacer beads play an important role in a piece by separating beads that are integral to the design. Although any bead can be a spacer bead, spacer beads must always be complementary to the design, even to the point of being unnoticed. Seed beads are acceptable spacers. Flat beads or discs, made of glass, metal, horn, and bone, are also good spacers.

Spacer Beads

Spacing Bars

Bali silver spacers, also known as daisy spacer beads, are very popular. These beads are covered with little bumps, also called beads, and nest easily to produce different effects. This type of spacer helps bring a metal effect through a whole necklace and can give it continuity—otherwise, a metal clasp on an all-glass strand may conflict with the design.

CRIMPS

One way to form a terminal is with a combination of beading wire and metal beads called crimp beads.

To use a crimp bead, string it on the wire and flatten it. For most uses the wire is crimped into a loop and usually incorporates the clasp. The loop creates the terminal end of the piece.

FORMING A LOOP TERMINAL

The simplest way to form a loop terminal is to string a crimp bead on the wire, pass the wire through the loop of the clasp and pass back through the crimp bead (Loop Terminal Figure A).

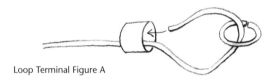

Loop Terminal Figure A

You want a loose fit that allows the loop to move easily around the clasp's loop. Make the loop about ⅛" long.

HOW TO CRIMP

1. At the end of a piece, string the crimp bead onto the beading wire, pass through one side of your clasp and pass back through the crimp bead.
2. Hold the beading wire in place by pinching it below the crimp bead with your fingers about ⅛" away from the end of the loop.
3. Place the crimping pliers over the crimp bead so that it rests in the second notch. Before you crimp the bead, check the size of the loop. Move the bead up or down the wire until the loop is the right size (Crimping Figure A).

4. Gently but firmly squeeze the pliers to pinch the crimp bead onto the wires. Ideally, each section of wire will rest on the opposite sides of the bead, with the center pinched down between them. However, this does not always happen—but follow the next step before you panic!

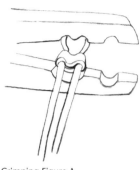

Crimping Figure A

5. Place the crimped wire in the next groove of the pliers and squeeze gently. This step rounds and reshapes the body of the crimp bead (Crimping Figure B).

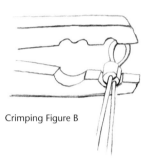

Crimping Figure B

6. Tug on the loop to be sure it is crimped securely. You can continue to shape the crimp bead by pinching it with the pliers at different angles. Shape any rough edges with a needle file.

At first, your crimp beads may not end up perfectly round, and the wires may not lie on each side of the crimp bead as they do in illustrations. Do not be discouraged. It takes practice, but a finished crimp also does not need to be perfectly round. As long as the bead is reasonably secure, blends in well with the piece, and is smooth with no sharp edges that will scratch the wearer, the crimp is fine.

If crimping makes you nervous, crimp a number of crimp beads onto two lengths of wire until you are comfortable crimping. The practice is worth the time and cost.

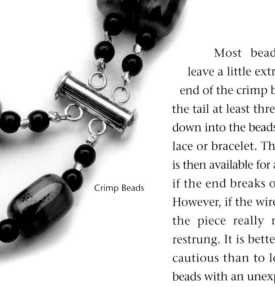

Crimp Beads

Crimp Tubes

Most beaders like to leave a little extra wire at the end of the crimp bead, tucking the tail at least three beads back down into the beads of the necklace or bracelet. This extra wire is then available for a quick repair if the end breaks or wears out. However, if the wire is breaking, the piece really needs to be restrung. It is better to be overcautious than to lose precious beads with an unexpected break.

If the holes of your beads are too small for the wire tail, trim the tail next to the crimp bead. Be careful not to cut or stress the wire you've strung beads on. Use wire cutters with a sharp edge. Cutters that are worn tend to pinch off the wire, leaving a rough edge. Wire that is cut cleanly will not scratch the wearer's skin.

CRIMP TUBES

Crimp tubes are a type of crimp bead that are smooth and shaped like cylinders. They work in the same way a crimp bead does.

Sterling Silver Tubes

Sterling silver crimp tubes have a sleek look. You can also use chain-nose pliers to flatten sterling crimp tubes; sterling is relatively soft and easy to pinch closed.

1. Move the tips of the chain-nose pliers over the

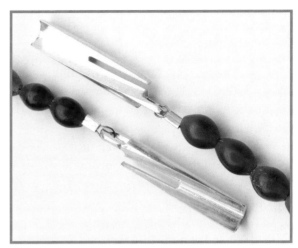

Sterling Silver Crimp Tubes

crimp tube until the width of the tube is covered by the width of the pliers' tips.
2. Hold in place and pinch firmly.

Lining up the chain-nose pliers with the width of the tube ensures that the finished tube will have no dents or marks.

Crimps With Attached Jump Ring

Some crimp tubes have jump rings attached. You crimp these tubes over the end of a wire as you do with other

Crimp Tubes with Attached Jump Ring

crimps, but without the loop terminal of the necklace. This crimp is a great choice for heavy wires because it caps the end of the wire but you don't have to fold the wire into a loop. To use these crimps with fine wire, add a seed bead to help anchor the crimp. You will need beading wire, a seed bead, and a crimp tube with attached jump ring.

1. Pass the end of the wire through the crimp bead, string a seed bead, and pass back through the crimp bead (Crimp with Anchor Figure A).

2. Pull the wire tight so that the seed bead rests at the top of the crimp and does not interfere with the jump ring.

3. Crimp with the crimping pliers, being careful to not break or stress the seed bead.

Crimp with Anchor Figure A

ADDING BULLION

To camouflage beading wire, you can use bullion, which is a very fine coil of silver wire. It is delicate, so handle it gently. Bullion cuts easily with wire cutters.

1. Cut the length of bullion you want and string it on the wire as if it were a bead. Keep it from passing into the crimp bead, but let it pass through the loop of the clasp.

2. Bend the beading wire and crimp as explained on page 44.

Covered Crimp

SAFETY CRIMP

If you are using heavy beads, such as a stone or lampworked ones, you can add a second or even third crimp as backup.

1. String one crimp just before the last bead. String the last bead and the second crimp bead. Add the clasp and a length of bullion if desired.

2. Pass back through all of the beads and pull snug. Trim the wire between the beads.

3. Crimp each bead as explained on page 44.

CLASPS

For most bracelet and necklace designs, you need some way to hold the two ends together. You will use several components to make and complete these closures—the jewelry's terminals, combined with connectors and a clasp.

The clasp is the "crown" of any necklace or bracelet—the final part that gives it life and function. The clasp need not be an integral part of the design, but it can be. Most of all, it needs to work smoothly and hold the piece together securely, but still allow the piece to be removed easily.

MANUFACTURED CLASPS

Most clasps have loops on which you attach the clasp to the beadwork. The specific design of each clasp varies, but most clasps have the same basic parts—a

Basic Clasp

hook, an eye ring or catch, and bails or loops. The hook is on one piece, the catch is on the other, and they link together to hold the piece in place.

Fishhook Clasp

This clasp comes in many different styles, but all work in the same way: The hook fits into the loop on the other side of the clasp. The clasp often has a ring at one end to attach it to the jewelry.

Fishhook Clasp

Fishhook Crimp Clasp

This clasp's loop forms the crimp terminal. Slide the end of the wire through the crimp, with the end coming out the other side about an inch. Crimp with a crimping pliers, but use only the rounding eye of the pliers. Firmly tug on the wire to see if it moves. If it does, crimp again.

When the crimp is secure, round and smooth out any dents or rough edges with the rounding eye of the crimping pliers. Use a file to smooth. Trim the wire.

Fishhook Crimp Clasp

Fishhook Clasp with Spring Catch

The catch on this clasp is pushed aside and the split ring slides over the hook. Attach a jump ring to both a terminal and the clasp bail. Attach a split ring to the opposite terminal to make the eye ring.

Fishhook Clasp with Spring Catch

Bayonet Clasp

One end of this clasp slides inside the other; the tension of the wire keeps it secured. Use it with pieces that do not have a lot of weight.

Bayonet Clasp

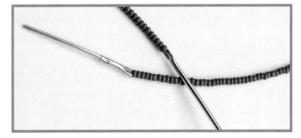

To attach the clasp, you simply crimp it onto the wire. Place a drop of G-S Hypo Cement glue on one end of the beading wire. With the clasp closed, slide the end of the beading wire into the open end of the clasp. Use chain-nose pliers to pinch the end of the clasp onto the wire. Be sure to wipe any excess glue off the clasp and pliers. Repeat with the other end of the wire, using tweezers to hold the wire as you crimp.

Sister Hook Clasp

This clasp consists of two fishhook shapes riveted so they slide open and closed in opposite directions. The eye ring is usually a split ring held in place by the weight of the necklace, and keeps the clasp closed. To open it, slide the jump ring out of the way and open the hooks.

Sister Hook Clasp

This sample is made with a split ring and crimp terminal. Any terminal with jump rings will work. The rivet holding the hooks together forms the clasp's ring bail.

"S" Hook Clasp

This clasp has a fishhook at each end, but one of the hooks is pushed closed so that it forms a loop. Each end of the clasp has a split ring for the piece's terminal.

"S" Hook Clasp

Fold-Over Clasp

The two parts of this clasp fit together by folding (Fold-Over Clasp Figure A). The top half is pushed down until it "snaps" over the bottom half. The tension of the pieces fitting together holds the clasp in place. Its compact design makes it ideal for bracelets. Even the most active person will have trouble snagging this clasp on clothing or objects.

Fold-Over Clasps

Fold-Over Clasp Figure A

Multiple-Strand Fold-Over Clasp

You can secure three strands (for example, three necklace strands) with this clasp. To attach the strands to the fold-over terminal, use a stop bead that rests on

Multiple-Strand Fold-Over Clasp

Box Clasps

Lobster Claw Clasp

the inside of the terminal. Secure the strand's wire with a crimp bead; secure the thread with a knot (Fold-over Clasp Figure A).

Box Clasp

Styles of box clasps vary widely, but they all work the same way. A box clasp has a hollow-shaped piece with an opening for a strip of metal that has been folded over to form a tongue. The tension in the folded metal forces the corresponding notches in both clasp pieces into place. Attach the terminal to the clasp's rings or loops at each end of the box clasp.

When you're using a box clasp for a multiple-strand piece, it is important to make sure that the jump rings do not interfere with the working of the catch.

Lobster Claw Clasp

This clasp has loops soldered at the base to attach to the terminal. The clasp has a hook with a lever that moves inside the body of the clasp to hold the clasp closed. To open, pull the lever button down. The spring automatically closes the ring to secure the clasp.

Pearl Clasp

This clasp combines the principles of both a fishhook clasp and a locking box mechanism. If the locking mechanism fails, the hook still catches itself on the clasp and does not come undone (Pearl Clasp Figure A).

Pearl Clasp

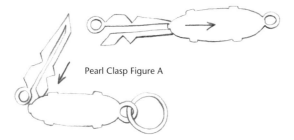
Pearl Clasp Figure A

Spring Ring Clasp

This common clasp is a circle formed by a tube with a slit running along the outer edge. The lever is set inside the tube to complete the circle. The lever button slides the spring and lever back along the slit to form an opening; slide an eye ring in and release the lever. Once released, the lever completes the circle and catches the eye ring inside. Spring rings are especially nice when used with tags—small, flat catches.

The spring ring has a jump ring at the base; use a jump ring between this clasp ring and the terminal. Use a jump ring or tag ring as an eye ring.

Toggle Clasps

These clasps have an eye ring and a bar. The bar is larger than the eye. To fasten the clasp, turn the toggle sideways and pass it through the eye. Once it's through, turn the toggle again so that it hooks on the eye, using the weight of the piece to keep the mechanism in place. The eye ring has a jump ring soldered at the base for attaching to the jewelry.

When you're using this clasp, make sure that the beads approaching the terminal are small enough that the bar can run completely through the eye. Sometimes, especially with shorter items like bracelets, the bead strand at the terminal leaves an undesirable gap between the jewelry and the clasp.

Spring Ring Clasps

Toggle Clasps

Barrel and Torpedo Clasps

The tube-shaped pieces of this clasp screw together to close. They come with head pin loops at each end that can be replaced or altered for different effects.

Torpedo clasps are like slender, long barrel clasps.

Barrel Clasp

Slide Clasp

The two halves of this clasp are sized so that one fits inside the other by sliding into place (Slide Clasp Figure A). Some slides have a tension wire to help secure them; some snap in place.

Slide Clasp Figure A

Slide Clasp

Lariat Clasp

This clever little clasp, uses both a loop and a toggle. One end of the piece slides down though the loop of the other half. The weight of the end holds it in place; a stopper bead strung along the cord keeps it from tightening up around the neck.

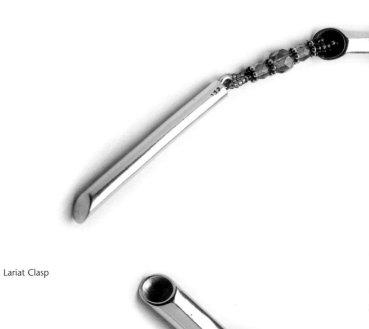

Lariat Clasp

Buckle Clasp

These clasps resemble belt buckles. A half tube or piece of bent metal hooks around a bar on the opposite side. The weight of the beadwork keeps the locking mechanism in place; however, locking also requires resistance between the body of the buckle and the parts. Without enough resistance, the slightest movement up or down will make it come undone. Buckle clasps are easy to use but not for active wear.

Lanyard Clasp

A lanyard clasp is a removable hook clasp. Most commonly, they are found on key chains and zipper pulls.

Use head pins or wire to attach a single large bead, pendant, or combination of beads to the lanyard clasp's bail. This decorative dangle can then be added and removed easily.

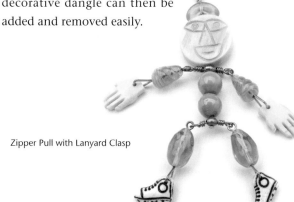

Zipper Pull with Lanyard Clasp

Assorted clasps.
Key: J = Jess Imports, C = Carl Clasmeyer, B = Burkett Studios, V = vintage, M = mass produced.

DESIGNER CLASPS

Designer clasps have a range of styles and types that is getting better every year. Many of the clasps available today are works of art in themselves, often too delightful to hide at the back of the neck. Some are worthy of being a centerpiece.

There are two general types of designer clasps. The first class, represented by the work of Burkett Studios and Carl Clasmeyer, are designed and manufactured by the artists themselves. The price range for these clasps is higher than other designer clasps, but they're worth the extra expense for the panache they add to any piece of jewelry.

The second kind of designer clasps costs less than the first kind but more than mass-produced ones. These clasps are usually designed by individual artists who then oversee production done by companies that specialize in producing a larger quantity than one artist can handle.

CLASPS TO MAKE

Creating your own clasp is an excellent way to make function and style work together. Making your own clasp takes more time than using a manufactured one, but it will match the beads and colors of a piece perfectly.

Two-Hole Bead Clasp

This is a good way to combine wire and beads. The clasp is formed with wire, while a bead forms both the base of the clasp and the terminal of the jewelry.

Two-Hole Bead Clasp

For this clasp, you need two 8mm beads with two holes and flat backs. You also need 8" of 20-gauge wire, round-nose pliers, wire cutters, and flat-nose pliers.

Catch

1. Cut 4" of wire. Bend a loop in the center, crossing the wire over itself (Two-Hole Bead Clasp Figure A).

2. Bend the wire back up around the point of the pliers. Flip the points of the pliers to the other side and repeat on the opposite side (Two-Hole Bead Clasp Figure B).

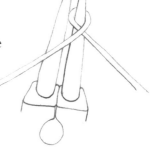

Two-Hole Bead Clasp Figure A

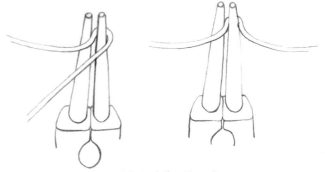

Two-Hole Bead Clasp Figure B

3. Trim ends to 1½ times the width of the bead (Two-Hole Bead Clasp Figure C).

4. Use flat-nose pliers to bend the ends of the wires toward each other (Two-Hole Bead Clasp Figure D).

Two-Hole Bead Clasp Figure C   Two-Hole Bead Clasp Figure D

5. Set the ends of the wire on either side of the bead so they are just inside the first hole. Using round-nose pliers, put one point into the loop and push into the wire with the other point. The wire will arc and tighten the points of the terminal into the holes (Two-Hole Bead Clasp Figure E).

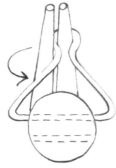

Two-Hole Bead Clasp Figure E

Hook

Work the hook following the same steps; however, make the loop formed in Step1 1½" long (Two-Hole Bead Clasp Figure F). Once the clasp is set, bend the hook down with round-nose pliers. Tilt the very tip of the hook up slightly (Two-Hole Bead Clasp Figure G).

Two-Hole Bead Clasp Figure F

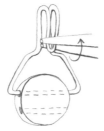

Two-Hole Bead Clasp Figure G

Jigged Wire Clasp

For this clasp, you need 20-gauge color-coated wire, a manufactured peg wire jig, a wire cutter, a file, and a permanent marker in a color that matches the wire.

1. Set the pegs according to the dots in Figure A.
2. Leaving a short tail, wrap the wire around the pegs, starting at the arrow on the chart and working around the pegs (Jigged Clasp Figure A).

Jigged Wire Clasp

3. Adjust the pegs. Bend the second half of the clasp, starting at the arrow (Jigged Clasp Figure B).
4. Use nylon-jaw pliers to pinch the wire, tightening up the loops and tempering the wire. You can wrap the wire, too, but wrap it gently so that it does not distort.
5. Trim the loops at both the start and end points. Loop them together and trim the wire to finish off each loop. Use the marker to color the ends if they are distracting.
6. Use the loops at each end to attach your beadwork.

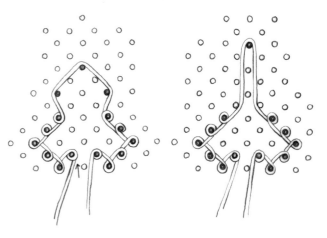

Jigged Clasp Figure A

Jigged Clasp Figure B

Peyote-Stitched Bracelet with Macaroni/Donut Toggle Clasp

Using seed beads and peyote stitch, you can make this clasp to complement the color and style of beads in a bracelet or necklace. Its unusual three-dimensional shape gives it a stylish flair that can make even a simple piece extraordinary.

Bracelet with Macaroni/Donut Toggle Clasp

You can attach this toggle clasp to any type of wide bracelet or necklace. I recommend a strap that is at least half as wide as the clasp. You can work the strap separately and sew this clasp to it; you can also use the clasp as the foundation for your needle weaving or multiple strands. To use the clasp as a foundation, make both halves of the clasp first. When attaching the toggle to your bracelet or necklace strap,

be sure to include enough beads in the stem of the toggle for it to go through the catch easily.

For the clasp, you will need Japanese 11° seed beads, a size 12 beading needle, and 4 yards of Spider-line Fusion beading thread.

Macaroni Toggle, Flat Peyote Stitch

1. String 12 beads. Work 3 rows of peyote stitch. (For peyote stitch instructions, see page 108.)
2. Work 3 rows, alternating between 1 and 2 beads for each set. Weave through several beads to secure (Macaroni Toggle Figure A).

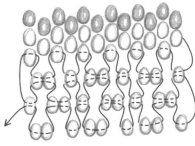

Macaroni Toggle Figure A

3. Beginning at the opposite side, work 3 rows of peyote stitch in 1- and 2-bead sets.
4. Work the last row using 2 beads in each set (Macaroni Toggle Figure B).
5. To close the toggle, weave the thread between the beads of the first and last rows, weaving back and forth like a zipper. Weave thread through several beads to secure (Macaroni Toggle Figure B).

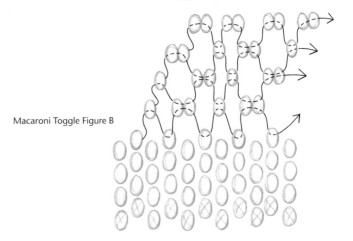

Macaroni Toggle Figure B

Peyote Donut Catch, Round Peyote Stitch

Rounds 1 and 2: Using 2 yards of Spiderline Fusion, string 24 beads. Pass through the first bead of the 24 to close the circle.

Rounds 3–8: Working clockwise, complete 6 rounds of peyote stitch. Be sure to keep track of your step-up beads.

Rounds 9 and 10: Work two rounds, increasing one bead every other stitch.

Round 11: Beginning with an increase, alternate stitches as in the previous two rounds.

Round 12: Work the round in two-drop peyote stitch. Weave through several beads and trim the thread. Remove the first two rounds.

Rounds 13 and 14: Work two rounds, increasing every other stitch.

Round 15: Beginning with an increase alternate stitches as in the previous two rounds.

Round 16: Sew the edges together by passing through the alternating beads of each row.

Square-Stitched Toggle Clasp

If peyote stitch is not your preferred stitch, try this square-stitched toggle. For square stitch instructions, see page 111. You will need seed beads, beading thread, and a beading needle.

Catch

Round 1: String 24 beads and tie into a circle. Square-stitch all around, working with two beads at a time. Pass through the first set to close the row. You now have a 2-round base circle.

Round 2A: String 3 beads and work the last 2 beads onto 2 beads of the first circle. Work all around the circle (Square-Stitched Toggle Clasp Figure A).

Square-Stitched Toggle Clasp

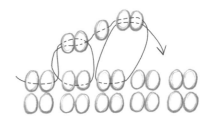

Square-Stitched Toggle Clasp Figure A

Rounds 2B and 3B: Pass down through the beads so you exit from the first round of the base circle. String 3 beads and work the last 2 beads onto 2 beads of the first round. Work all around the circle so you end up with two layers of beadwork off the base circle.

Outside Round 5: Square-stitch this row to Row 3, skipping every 3rd bead of Row 3. (Square-Stitched Toggle Clasp Figure B).

Square-Stitched Toggle Clasp Figure B

Toggle

1. Begin your thread by exiting from 1 bead at the end of the jewelry piece. String 11 beads (Square-Stitched Toggle Clasp Figure C).

Square-Stitched Toggle Clasp Figure C

2. Square-stitch 3 rows, working two beads at a time (Square-Stitched Toggle Clasp Figure D).

Square-Stitched Toggle Clasp Figure D

3. Once the rows are complete, sew Row 1 to Row 3. (Square-Stitched Toggle Clasp Figure E).

Square-Stitched Toggle Clasp Figure E

4. Sew Row 4 to Row 2 on the opposite side (Square-Stitched Toggle Clasp Figure F).

5. Pass through the beads to the center set of any row. String enough beads to equal about half the length of the toggle. Attach this length of beads to the end of a strap bracelet, passing through several times to reinforce for strength.

Square-Stitched Toggle Clasp Figure F

Lariat Necklace with Self-Clasp

Make a lariat necklace with single-needle right-angle weave, another stitch you prefer, or simply with a strand of large beads. For the clasp, you will need seed beads, beading thread, and a beading needle.

Working off the last bead at one end of the necklace, make a loop of seed beads that is big enough to loosely fit around the diameter of the rest of the necklace. Use any stitch you like to work rows of seed beads to form a tube. Embellish the tube with fringe or decorative

Lariat Necklace with Self-Clasp, closed

beads as desired. The pictured clasp shows a tube made of single-needle right-angle weave.

You can add other embellishments: fringe along the side and bottom of the tube, or a right-angle weave tail at the tip of the second end.

To use, just pass the other end of the necklace through the embellished loop.

Lariat Necklace with Self-Clasp, open

Sling Clasp Bracelet

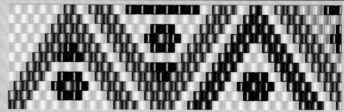

This clever little clasp is slightly awkward to close, but it is so secure that even the most active person can wear it. Two strips of flat peyote make up the slings that hold the toggle and form a very stylish clasp.

Materials

Magnifica beads in the following colors:

7g base color—cream-11087

2g khaki-11072

2g pale salmon-11051

2g golden ginger-11015

2g accent color—brown-11066

Beading thread

Notions

Size 12 beading needle

Scissors

First, work the bracelet strap in flat peyote stitch following the graph (Sling Clasp Figure A). For flat peyote stitch instructions, see page 108. Alternate making the V shapes in the 3 colors. Repeat 3 times and work the rest of the strap in cream.

Catch

1. Once you have the length you want, work 24 rows of cream on one side of the strap using 2 beads per row. Secure thread.

2. Begin a new thread at the other side of the strap, and weave 24 rows as before (Sling Clasp Figure B).

3. String 4 beads between the end of the second loop strap and the first one.

4. Weave 7 rows, working the whole width of the strap.

5. Sew the end down along the eighth row from the end of the strap. Secure the end (Sling Clasp Figure C).

Toggle

1. String 14 beads. Using flat peyote stitch, weave 6 more rows, with 7 beads per row, for a total of eight rows. Sew the last row of beads onto the first row of beads.

2. Weave to the middle of the toggle. String four beads and attach to the bracelet. Weave back toward the toggle, working flat peyote stitch on the 4 beads to strengthen (Sling Clasp Figure D).

Sling Clasp Figure B

Sling Clasp Figure C

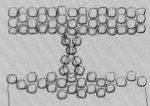

Sling Clasp Figure D

Beaded Loop Clasp

This clasp is a great way to feature a distinctive button or bead. For this technique, you need seed beads to match your piece, and a button or large bead for the clasp.

Loop

1. Using a thread that is securely attached to the end of your beaded piece, work your way to the last bead in the center of the beadwork. Create a stem by stringing 1 or more beads to separate the loop from the beadwork. Add decorative beads or a little length to the piece in the stem if you wish.

2. String the number of beads necessary to create a loop that slips easily around the width of the button or bead you will use as a catch. Pass back down through the stem and into the end of the beadwork. Pass through all—the stem, the loop, and back down into the piece—one or more times to strengthen the loop. Weave back into the body of the beadwork and secure.

Catch

1. Securely attach a thread at the opposite end of the piece. Exit from a center bead in the piece. Create a stem for the catch by stringing 1 or more beads—in most cases, you will need at least 2 beads to create enough room between the catch and the beadwork for the loop to rest securely. If the catch is too crowded, the loop will not sit correctly against the bead.

Beaded Loop Clasp

2. *For a button catch:* After creating the stem, pass the needle through the holes or the shank, adding seed beads to disguise the thread, if desired. Pass back through the stem and into the beadwork. Pass through all—the stem, the button, and the piece— one or more times to strengthen. Weave back into the body of the beadwork and secure the thread.

For a bead catch: Pass through the large bead. Add a stop bead and pass down through the large bead, through the stem, and through the end of the beadwork. Pass through all—the stem, the bead, and the piece—one or more times to strengthen. Weave back into the body of the beadwork and secure the thread.

Pomegranate Stitch Bracelet with Geometric Clasp

Pomegranate Stitch Bracelet with Geometric Clasp

This "pomegranate stitch" is a combination of daisy chain, square stitch, and single-needle right-angle weave. (See page 108 for a description of these techniques.) Combining the stitches creates an interesting fabric with a three-dimensional aspect that is appealing as much for the way it feels as for the look it creates. The catch uses a specific count to make it round, but the rest of the bracelet is worked with the same patterns or "rhythms" as any right-angle weave piece.

Materials
1 tube 11° Japanese seed beads
½ tube 8° seed beads
Beading thread

Notions
Size 12 beading needle
Scissors

1. String 24 beads. Pass through all again and tie a knot to close the circle.

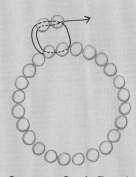

Pomegranate Bracelet Figure A

2. Square-stitch 2 beads at a time around the circle (Pomegranate Bracelet Figure A). Pass through the first 2-bead set to close the round. Pass through the corresponding 2-bead set of the bottom round, to turn in the opposite direction (Pomegranate Bracelet Figure B).

3. String 8 beads and pass back through the 2-bead set in the opposite direction. Pull tight to form a loop. Pass through the 2-bead set of the top row (Pomegranate Bracelet Figure C).

4. Coming out of the 2-bead set of the top row, square-stitch 2 beads at a time onto the bottom loop just formed. Pass through the top 2-bead set (the leg).

5. String an 8° bead. Pass through the center of the working circle. From the back side of the loop, pass through the 4 beads of the bottom row. You have worked the crossover bead (Pomegranate Bracelet Figure D).

6. String 6 beads. Pass through the next 2 beads of the bottom row of the circle and up through the leg of the last loop. Pass down the top 2 beads of the leg and through the next 2 beads of the circle (Pomegranate Bracelet Figure E).

7. Square-stitch 3 sets of 2 beads at a time on the loop. Pass back through the leg and 2 beads of the circle. Work the crossover bead.

Pomegranate Bracelet Figure B

Pomegranate Bracelet Figure C

Pomegranate Bracelet Figure D

Pomegranate Bracelet Figure E

8. Repeat Steps 6 and 7 around the circle until you have 2 beads left.

9. To work the last set, string 4 beads. Pass through the two adjacent legs and 2 beads of the circle to form the bottom rung. Pass through the top legs and the 2 beads of the inner circle. Bring the thread up to the outer edge to begin stitching again (Pomegranate Bracelet Figure F).

Pomegranate Bracelet Figure F

10. Square-stitch 2 sets of 2 beads at a time onto the 4 bead sets (each 4-bead set is a "ring") along the outer edge. Pass down the top leg and through the 2 beads of the circle. Work the crossover bead (Pomegranate Bracelet Figure G). Working

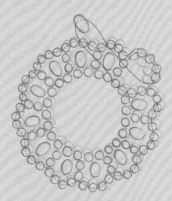

Pomegranate Bracelet Figure G

around the outer edge, pass through the beads of the rungs. Continue passing through on both the top and the bottom until the bead centers feel full of thread. These passes will stiffen the edges of the clasp.

Strap

The rows of the strap make its length; you add the second row below the first row and the third row above the first row (Pomegranate Strap Figure A).

Pomegranate Strap Figure A

Row 1

1. Working off the edge of the catch you just made, string 6 beads. Pass back through the 2 beads of the edge of the catch (Pomegranate Strap Figure B).

Pomegranate Strap Figure B

2. Square-stitch 2 beads at a time along the 6 beads just added. Pass through the top 2 beads on the catch and work a crossover bead.

3. Working off the 2 beads, repeat the process for your desired length (Pomegranate Strap Figure C).

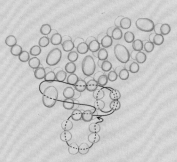

Pomegranate Strap Figure C

Row 2

1. Weave to the top 2-bead set along the first row. String 6 beads and pass back through the 2 beads of the last row (Pomegranate Strap Figure D).

2. Square-stitch 2 beads at a time on the 6 beads just added. Pass through the 2 beads of the last row and through the first 2 beads of the square stitch. Work the crossover bead (Pomegranate Strap Figure E).

3. String 4 beads. Pass through 4 bottom beads (2 of the last row and 2 of

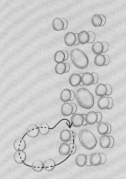

Pomegranate Strap Figure D

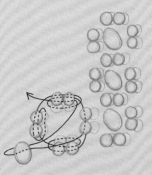

Pomegranate Strap Figure E

Pomegranate Stitch Bracelet with Geometric Clasp

one more set in the center. (Pomegranate Toggle Figure A).

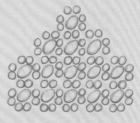

Pomegranate Toggle Figure A

1. Using the pomegranate stitch again, make a short row of 5 sets. Pass the needle around the outer edges of the row, adding a seed bead between the sets to fill in gaps. This pass will square up and stiffen the toggle. Pass through the outer edge again if needed.

2. Bring the thread out of the center set of the toggle. String beads between the toggle and the end of the strap. Pass through them again to secure and reinforce (Pomegranate Toggle Figure B). Note that the length of beads between the toggle and the strap should be slightly longer than the toggle so the clasp will fit together easily.

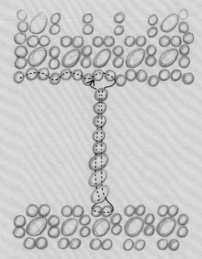

Pomegranate Toggle Figure B

the last set of the working row). Pass back down through the corresponding top beads.

4. Square-stitch 2 beads at a time onto the 4 beads just added. Pass through the 2 beads of the last set to close the row. Work a crossover bead and pass through the next 2-bead set of the last row.

5. Repeat along the edge of the last row.

Toggle

For a simple straight end, just add the toggle as described below. For a tapered end, first add a bead set to the center row and then add the toggle. If the bracelet is 5 rows wide, add 3 bead sets in the center, and then finish with

Peyote Bracelet with Bent Wire Created Clasp

Peyote Bracelet with Bent Wire Created Clasp

Bent wire is an excellent tool for creating your own slide clasp. You make the hook with wire and the catch with seed beads.

Materials
Magnifica seed beads in the following colors:
7g cream-11010
2g pink-11025
2g bronze-11012
2g red-11033
2g brown-11019
2g orange-11031
2g purple-11020
2g blue-11021
Beading thread

Notions
Size 12 beading needle

Weave the bracelet strap using peyote stitch, following the graph (Bent Wire Clasp Figure A). Use the stripes graphed at one end to lengthen or shorten the bracelet.

Clasp
1. Cut a 4" length of 14-gauge wire. NOTE: 14-gauge wire is sharper when cut than smaller-gauge wire.

Bent Wire Clasp Figure A→

To avoid scratching or cutting your fingers, sand the ends of the wire with a medium-grit sanding block each time you cut.

2. Using the wide end of the tips of round-nose pliers, bend the wire in a U shape 1" from the end—or at a point slightly farther from the end than the width of the bracelet. Curve the end slightly with the tips of the round-nose pliers. On the opposite side, 1" from the bend, bend again and use round-nose pliers to create a spiral or other shape with the rest of the wire (Bent Wire Clasp Figure B).

Bent Wire Clasp Figure B

3. Sew one end of the strap to the wire clasp. Fold the end over the wire and pass the needle through the beads of the last row and the eighth row from the end. Position the wire shape into a pleasing position (Bent Wire Clasp Figure C).

4. Sew the last row of the opposite end to the eighth row from the end to form a tube (Bent Wire Clasp Figure D). Reinforce the beadwork and secure the thread. Slide the end of the clasp into the tube. If the clasp does not fit easily, trim the end.

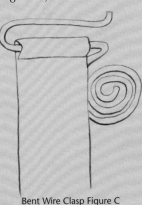

Bent Wire Clasp Figure C

Once the clasp slides in and out of the tube easily—but still stays in place—file or sand the end smooth.

EAR WIRES

You can make an infinite variety of earrings with manufactured and created ear wires. The examples here are a small fraction of what is possible. Some are standards; some are new twists on an old theme. Learning the basics is necessary, but do not restrict your imagination.

MANUFACTURED EAR WIRES

An excellent selection of ear wires is available on the market today, including French hooks, kidney wires, and posts. Each type comes in various shapes and sizes; some even have fancy decorations. They also come in a variety of materials, including sterling and even plastic.

Using Wire Hoops

Here are a couple of ways to embellish wire hoops. Use them as a jumping-off point for your own unique creation.

Bead Assortments

Hold the hoop open with your thumb and index finger. Slide the beads onto the hoop. Use round-nose pliers to slightly bend up the end. Use a cup burr to smooth the end of the wire (Wire Hoops Figure A).

Wire Hoops Figure A

Flowers

Use a crimp bead to hold the beads steady on the wire. Crimp bead and crimp it in the 5 o'clock position, toward the back of the hoop. Add seed beads, a leaf, and a flower; use a single black seed bead for the flower center. Finish the end of the wire.

Ear Wire Hoops: Frogs

Ear Wire Hoops: Flowers

Using Crimp Hoops

1. Open up the hoop and slide the beads on.
2. Put the end of the wire hoop back in place. Using chain-nose pliers, pinch the crimp closed (Crimp Hoops Figure A).
3. Make 2 hoops and add to ear wires.

Crimp Hoops

Crimp Hoops Figure A

Using and Embellishing Kidney Wires

Embellish kidney wires with beads or off-loom stitches. Add a beaded dangle and close the bottom loop.

Kidney Wires   Embellished Kidney Wires

Brick-Stitched Hoops

Rainbow Ruffle
Embellished
Wire Hoops

20 Picots Embellished
Wire Hoops

Using off-loom beadwork to embellish wire hoops is a great way to add delicate colors and patterns to a simple piece of jewelry. These earrings do not take a large amount of time or beads, and they are an ideal way to practice basic stitches and combine a variety of stitches.

Hook-Stitched Hoops

Materials

A small assortment of seed beads

Beading thread in a complementary color

Round hoop earrings about 1" in diameter

Notions

Size 12 beading needle

Scissors

Hook-Stitched Hoops
Figure A

1. Work a row of hook stitch along the wire (Hook-Stitched Hoops Figure A). For hook stitch instructions, see page 108.

2. *To make an increase* string 3 beads. Work the hook stitch using the last 2 beads of the 3 just added (Hook-Stitched Hoops Figure B).

4. Square-stitch the beads together to keep them tight. Make more increases work in the same fashion (Hook-Stitched Hoops Figure C).

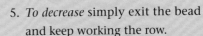

Hook-Stitched
Hoops Figure B

Hook-Stitched
Hoops Figure C

5. *To decrease* simply exit the bead and keep working the row.

6. When you're working around the arc of a hoop, you will end up with gaps. Gaps look acceptable if they are evenly spaced. Each set of beads will meet along the bottom of the sets next to the hoop. The tops will have a slight gap. You can use the gaps as part of the design by stringing beads on the thread between the sets (a rung) (Hook-Stitched Hoops Figure D).

7. To keep the sets standing up, pass though the very first set, passing the thread behind the ring bail of the hoop (Hook-Stitched Hoops Figure E). Add a bead as a dangle if you want the sets to droop away from the hoop (Hook-Stitched Hoops Figure F).

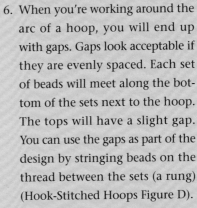

Hook-Stitched Hoops Figure D

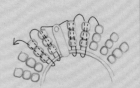

Hook-Stitched Hoops Figure E

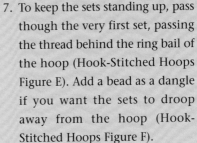

Hook-Stitched Hoops Figure F

20 Picots Hoop

Materials

1g of Magnificas in black-11003
1g of Magnificas in transparent gray-11069
1g of Magnificas in silver-lined -11001
Beading thread
Wire hoops 1" inch diameter

Notions

Size 12 beading needle
Scissors

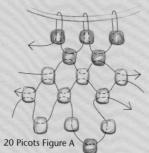

20 Picots Figure A

1. Work 20 picots along the wire hoop in black. (For picot instructions, see page 110.)
2. Work 2 rows of flat peyote stitch across the 20 rung beads of the picot using the transparent gray beads.
3. On the fourth row, alternate peyote stitches, using first 1 bead then a set of 3 beads. In the 3-bead sets, use a silver-lined bead for the second bead. This pattern creates a nice picot-style edge (20 Picots Figure A).

20 Picots Rainbow Ruffle Hoops

Materials

2g Magnificas in the following colors:
yellow-11043
orange-11119
red-11106
violet-11092
blue-11058
green-11045
Beading thread in a complementary color
2 wire hoops 1½" in diameter

Notions

Size 12 beading needle
Scissors

Using about 1½ yards of thread, tie the end of the thread onto the wire hoop.

Row 1: Work a 20-picot edging along the wire hoop with yellow beads.

Rows 2 and 3: Work 2 rows of flat peyote across the 20 "rung" beads of the picot with orange.

Row 4: String 3 red beads and pass through the next bead of the last row. Repeat along the row. On the last set, string 5 beads of the next row's color and pass the needle through the "point" bead (see below) of the last set worked in the row. These beads begin the next row.

Rows 5, 6, and 7: Work 3 rows of netting, using the point beads of the previous row. Work each row in the last 3 colors, as indicated in the graph. End each row with a 5-bead set that runs into the last set to begin a new row.

To end, pass the thread through the beads to the picot row. Knot the thread onto the thread lying along the hoop and secure.

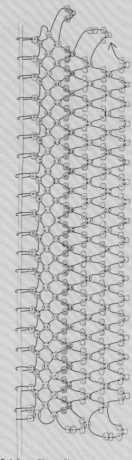

Rainbow Picots Figure A

TIPS FOR READING RAINBOW PICOTS FIGURE A
• The hoop is drawn straight to make the graph easier to read. The beads will actually be arced around the edge of the hoop.
• Start at the upper left-hand dot and work left to right. Work consecutive rows alternating between left to right and right to left.
• A "point" bead is the center bead in each set of netting.

Jigged Ear Wires

Materials

Two 20-gauge silver or gold 6" wires

Beaded dangle (made with a head pin
or beaded cabochon)

Notions

Delphi wire jig

Round-nose pliers

Wire cutters

½" starter stick

Sanding block or cup burr

Leather or nylon mallet

Nylon-jaw pliers

Jeweler's block or anvil

1. Place the pegs in the jig following the graph.
2. Bend a loop at one end of the wires. Place the loop on the first peg and then bend each wire around the pegs of the jig. Follow the graph for the direction of the bends (Jigged Earring Wires Figure A).

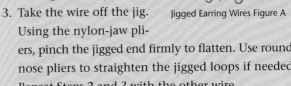

Jigged Earring Wires Figure A

3. Take the wire off the jig. Using the nylon-jaw pliers, pinch the jigged end firmly to flatten. Use round-nose pliers to straighten the jigged loops if needed. Repeat Steps 2 and 3 with the other wire.

4. Holding a jigged wire, use your thumb to hold the unjigged portion of the wire firmly against the starter stick. Bend the wire around the stick and then arc it over your index finger (Jigged Earring Wires Figure B). Bend the second wire. Hold them together, and bend them with your fingers to make the shapes match. Trim both ear wires even.

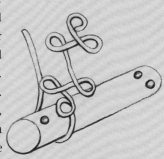

Jigged Earring Wires Figure B

5. Temper the wire part of the earring by laying it on the block or anvil and pounding with the leather or nylon mallet. As you work, remember to check the wires for strength; over-tempering will make them brittle. Use a sanding block or cup burr to smooth the ends.

6. Add the beaded dangle.

Two-Hole Bead Spirals

Materials List
8" of 20-gauge wire (Note: the wire
  needs to fit the holes of the beads;
  use whatever size works)
A small assortment of beads
Two 2-hole beads
Ear wires

Notions
Wire cutters
Round-nose pliers
File or sanding block

1. Cut the wire into two 4" lengths.
2. Bend the wire in the center.
3. Slide seed beads on each side. Slide a
   two-hole bead onto the wire ends. Add
   more seed beads on each side.
4. Trim the ends even. Sand the ends
   until they're smooth.
5. Bend the wire ends into spirals see
   page 111 for how to bend a spiral.
6. Add an ear wire.

Materials
7g of base color of Magnificas
2g of a second color of Magnificas
Larger bead for flower center
Silamide thread
24" of 22-gauge wire
1 pin back

Notions
Size 12 beading needle
Scissors

Brick-Stitched Flower Pin

1. Work a row of ladder stitch 16 beads long (or 2 beads for each petal desired). For
   ladder stitch instructions, see page 108. This your foundation row.
2. Brick-stitch points along the foundation in the desired colors or shapes. Do so
   by working a 2-bead row on the bridge of thread between 2 beads of the foundation row. Increase each consecutive row until you have a row of 5 beads. You
   can make longer, more interesting points by decreasing and increasing consecutive rows to lengthen the petals and by adding different color patterns as you
   work.
3. Once the petals are as long as you would like them, work brick stitch to create
   a point. On the last 2-bead row, string a single bead to complete the tip and
   weave through the beadwork until you reach the foundation row.
4. Work 8 petals on each side of the foundation row,
   repeating the combination of rows and color in each
   petal.
5. Sew the foundation's ends together and stitch the petals
   together just above the foundation row, working back
   and forth around the center between the petals.
6. Pass a 24" length of wire through a bead that will serve
   as the center of the flower. Push the bead to the center and bend the wire around (Brick-Stitched Flower
   Figure A). Pass through the center of the flower and
   bend each wire out.
7. Wrap the ends of the wire around the cross bar of a pin
   back. Finish the ends of the wire with complementary
   beads or by twisting the wire into scrolls (Brick-Stitched
   Flower Figure B).

Brick-Stitched Flower Figure A

Brick-Stitched Flower Figure B

PINS

A pin can be a soft, subtle accent or an outrageous and flamboyant statement. Whichever end of the spectrum you prefer, the essence of a pin is pleasure. They are as much fun to make as they are to wear.

Here are some basic instructions for using manufactured and created pin findings. In the Finishing section you will find detailed instructions for using them with beaded cabochons and backed beadwork.

SAFETY-TYPE PINS

You can make pins using large decorative "safety-pin" findings. Either slide beads onto the straight part of the pin or add dangles made from head pins. Some of these pins have loops soldered along the bottom from which you can suspend dangles.

Some safety-type pins are made so that the head screws off. Slide beads onto the body of the pin and replace the head.

CLUTCH PINS

Clutch pins are designed for making tie tacks, but you can use them for other

Safety-Type Pins

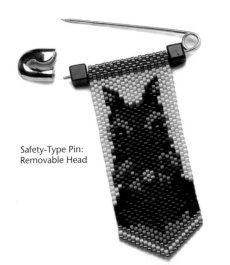

Safety-Type Pin: Removable Head

projects. You can attach beads to the flat button shape with epoxy; you can also glue a clutch finding to the underside of a cabochon before finishing it.

HAT PINS

Hat pin findings look like one long, tempered wire. You can use these findings in many ways: Glue beads on the end, thread beads onto the wire and hold them on by bending and shaping the wire, or glue flat beadwork onto the wire.

Making Pins from Hat Pin Findings

Because it is tempered, the wire designed for hatpins is excellent for making pins. To use other wires, you need to temper the wire to stiffen it.

1. Decide on the length of the pin. Bend the wire with round-nose pliers (Hat Pin as Finding Figure A).

Hat Pin as Pin Finding Figure A

2. Bend the catch up and then down with round-nose pliers. Trim the extra wire or bend a loop.
3. Bend the catch over.

Hat Pins

Hat Pins as Findings

FINISHINGS

Finishing a piece of jewelry is largely a matter of personal choice. An unlimited variety of techniques is available; some types of embellishment can serve as finishing techniques as well. The more techniques you master, the more choices you have for adding personality to your creations. Being able to incorporate many elements will help you create details that speak of quality and skill to even the most observant critic.

KNOTTING AND ANCHORING

No matter how proficient you are at beadwork, knots can be the most frustrating part of any project. They bring persistent, haunting concerns: Will you make a successful knot? Will it hold? Will it look clumsy? Practicing knots will give you confidence. A neatly tied knot does not detract from any work, even when it shows. Once you master knots, tying them properly brings a subtle sense of satisfaction.

Be sure to stretch cord before you use it or the weight of the beads will lengthen it. To stretch cord, gently tug along the entire length of cord until it is taut.

Lark's Head Knot

One way to attach cord to a clasp is with a lark's head knot.

1. Pass the end of the cord through the clasp ring.
2. Bring the cord around and to the back of the ring and then through in the opposite direction.
3. Bring the end of the cord down through the loop that forms (Lark's Head Knot Figure A). Finish the tail by gluing. Trim close when the knot is secure.

Lark's Head Knot Figure A

Half Hitch Knot

You can also attach a cord to a clasp with a series of half hitch knots.

1. Bring the end around the back and then across the front.
2. Pass the end through the loop that forms. Pull tight.
3. Repeat the half hitch 5 more times to form 3 double half hitches (Half Hitch Knot Figure A).

Half Hitch Knot Figure A

4. Add a drop of fabric glue and rub it into the fibers. Let it dry. Look closely to see if the end of the cord is secure. If not, add another drop of glue. Trim close when the end is secure.

MULTIPLE OVERHAND KNOTS

This series of knots forms a large, tapered knot. It's handy when you are using a lightweight cord with bead tips.

1. Wrap the cord around the index and middle finger and hold in place with the thumb. There should be a space between the two fingers inside the loop.
2. Wrap the cord around the anchored section 2 times. You can wrap even more times for a larger knot, but the more cord you add, the more difficult it is to finish the knot neatly (Multiple Overhand Knot Figure A).

Multiple Overhand Knot Figure A

3. Remove the middle finger from the loop and pinch the first wrap to hold the loop in place. Slide the end of the awl inside the loop. Pull the thread tight around the awl's point (Multiple Overhand Knot Figure B).

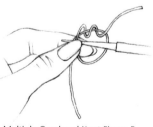

Multiple Overhand Knot Figure B

4. Lay the necklace out straight, making sure the beads are not kinked. Holding the end of the thread firmly, push the awl forward and slide the knot up to the mouth of the bead tip or bead hole (Multiple Overhand Knot Figure C).

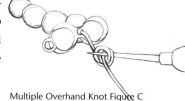

Multiple Overhand Knot Figure C

Multiple Overhand Knot
Figure D

5. Tilt the awl up with the point aiming at the center of the bead tip. Tighten the knot as you slide it down and off the tip (Multiple Overhand Knot Figure D).

ANCHORING A TAIL

Whereas knots are integral to the function and life span of a piece of jewelry, tails are, well, expendable. After you have tied a secure knot, you always have a tail of thread to deal with. It does not matter how much thread you weave into beadwork; eventually, you need to do something with the end of the thread.

It is the nature of tails to wag, whether on a dog or beadwork. I have seen fabulous bead artists embarrassed by an otherwise gorgeous piece of beadwork because a tail has worked its way out and is showing. Anchoring the tail reduces the chances of errant tails, and a few simple steps help you do so.

Burning a Tail

To end a thread, trim it to about ¼". Hold the tail up to a flame, just close enough to melt the end of the tail into a little bead of thread that serves to anchor the tail in place. I use a lighter, but a tool called Max Wax can do pinpoint thread burning.

To anchor a new thread in beadwork, first hold the long end of thread up to the flame to form an anchoring bead.

Gluing a Tail

Tie a half hitch knot and secure it with a drop of glue. I suggest G-S Hypo Cement. Trim the tail close when the glue is dry.

To anchor a new thread, tie it in a half hitch at the edge of the work onto the bridge threads between the beads. Place a drop of glue on the knot and let it dry. Pass the needle through several beads into the beadwork and begin working. Trim the tail.

ADDING AND ENDING THREADS IN BEADWORK

Adding and ending threads is an important beadworking skill that combines tying knots with anchoring tails.

In both large and small projects, unexpected things can happen—a snag frays the thread; a sharp-edged bead or a hard tug on a needle breaks the thread. These accidents make it necessary either to replace the thread or start over. The act of pulling long threads through each stitch can weaken the fibers of even the best thread. Rather than try to work every project with a thread more than a few yards long, you will better spend the time learning the skills of adding and ending threads.

Loomwork

To end threads on loomwork, tie a half hitch onto the edge warp thread at the end of the last row worked. Pass through the beads one row back. Tie a double half hitch. Pass back through the next row, stopping in the middle. Bring the thread out between the beads. At the end of the loomwork—once you have secured the warp threads and removed the work from the loom—anchor the tails by burning them.

Brick Stitch

To end thread on a brick-stitched piece, weave it back 3 beads. Double-stitch by passing through the second bead in the opposite direction. Tie a half hitch onto the bridge between the beads. Anchor and trim and the tail.

Square Stitch

To end square-stitched threads, weave through several of the beads. Tie a half hitch onto the bridge threads along the edge or between sets. Anchor and trim the thread.

You can add a new thread after anchoring the old thread. Anchor the old thread and pass through a few sets with the new thread. Tie a half hitch on the bridge threads. Pass through the beads where you want to start again and begin the square stitch.

To glue the new thread, tie a half hitch on the bridge threads and add a drop of glue. Work through the sets and rows to where you want to begin. Trim the tail when the glue is dry.

Peyote Stitch and Netting

To end a thread in peyote stitch and netting, tie a half hitch on the thread between the beads of the last row—the row you passed through when you were working the last bead.

Weave through several of the closest beads of the previous row. Remove the needle from the old thread and start a new thread.

To add a new thread, burn a knot on the end of the new thread. Pass through several beads and tie a half hitch knot between beads. Weave through beads to get to your last bead.

Right-Angle Weave

To end a thread in right-angle weave, pass through the last 4-bead set twice, tying a half hitch before and after one of the outside beads. Anchor the tail.

Backing

FINDINGS WITH BACKED BEADWORK

Adding a finding behind beadwork is a multistep process. Besides the metal finding, you also want to create a fabric backing to give your piece a finished look and to protect it and the wearer.

Using padding with your fabric backing provides a soft, luxurious texture while it covers threads and knots on the underside of the beadwork. If you incorporate wire findings on the back of your work, padding softens the wire's bumps and shapes and supports the backing so that the findings don't stress the fabric.

My preference for backing material is Lacy's Stiff Stuff and Ultrasuede. It is thick enough to pad the backing without being bulky. Here's how to do it.

1. Turn the beadwork over. If the piece includes fabric (such as a bead-embroidered piece), trim the fabric close to the stitching, making sure you do NOT cut any threads or fringe. If this process makes you nervous, use a strip of tape to hold the fringe up and away from the surface of the backing material.

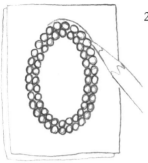

Backing Beadwork Figure A

Backing Beadwork Figure B

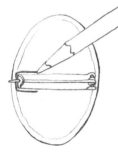

Backing Beadwork Figure C

Backing Beadwork Figure D

2. Adhere a piece of Stiff Stuff to a piece of Ultrasuede with a glue stick. Using the glue stick instead of glue prevents glue from soaking through the suede and making it stiff. The glue stick serves as the glue equivalent of basting, and the edging holds the layers together permanently. Both Stiff Stuff and Ultrasuede should be slightly larger than the beadwork.

3. Lay the beadwork over the Stiff Stuff with the Ultrasuede side down. With a pencil, lightly trace around the edges (Backing Beadwork Figure A). Cut the Ultrasuede just outside the traced line. Trim the edges of the Stiff Stuff along the inside of the pencil line (Backing Beadwork Figure B). The beadwork and Ultrasuede form a pocket that holds the backing together when you come to sew an edging.

4. Now add the finding—such as a pin back, barrette clip, tie tack, or earring post. Place the finding onto the prepared backing and trace the finding with a pencil (Backing Beadwork Figure C). For barrettes and pins, cut slits in the suede (Backing Beadwork Figure D). Place the finding so that it sticks out from the underside of the backing. For earring posts or tie tacks, poke a hole in the suede layers with an awl and insert the finding from the underside of the backing.

5. On the back of the beadwork, place a good-sized drop of fabric glue on the center only. Keeping the glue in the center helps prevent leaks at the edges; also, edging will be easier if you do not have to sew through glue. Press the Ultrasuede and backing onto the back (Backing Beadwork Figure E). Allow the glue to set according to manufacturer's directions.

Backing Beadwork Figure E

Overlapping Clasp

This clasp is made with fabric—Ultrasuede is particularly nice—and snaps or a hook-and-eye clasp of the type usually used in sewing. Making the clasp requires glue, backing or interfacing material, a beading needle, and scissors. You can attach it to pieces of finished loomwork or use it as a foundation for beading.

Overlapping Clasp

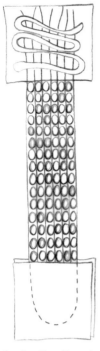

To make this clasp with loomwork, start before you cut the work off the loom.

1. While the work is on the loom, weave the working thread through the warp threads along the ends of the beads.
2. Glue squares of leather or Ultrasuede over and beneath the warp threads, lining up the edges at the end of the beads (Overlapping Clasp Figure A).
3. Once the glue is dry, cut the leather to shape and add button snaps or hook-and-eye clasps.

To use this clasp for a bead-embellished button closure, follow the instructions below.

1. Arrange 3 layers of backing—2 of the fabric and a middle layer of interfacing or backing material.

Overlapping Clasp Figure A

Overlapping Clasp Figure B

Overlapping Clasp Figure C

2. Sew the buttonhole.
3. Bead embellish the middle and top layers, working around the buttonhole and the spot where you want the button to be (Overlapping Clasp Figure B).
4. When the beadwork is complete, glue the layers together with flexible glue—I use Aleene's Flexible Stretchable Fabric Glue—and allow to dry following manufacturer's directions. Sew on the button (Overlapping Clasp Figure C).

Fringes and Edgings

EDGINGS AND FRINGES

A well-done edging or an unusual fringe can add the finishing touch to a jewelry piece that will really make it pop. The edging or fringe can be the crown of a perfect piece—or it can create a nagging sense that the piece is off. As with stitches and other techniques, the more edgings and fringes you are familiar with, the more professional your beadwork can look. No rules apply universally for all pieces; using these techniques is a matter of personal preference.

EDGINGS

Edgings add a polished or fancy look to many different styles of beadwork. Bead placement and thread paths for different types of edgings vary widely.

"Mandala" Edging

There is no rule to follow for my mandala edging; the number of beads used accounts for the look. You need seed beads, a beading needle, and beading thread.

Mandala Edging

The legs are the beads that come up and out from or into the edge of the beadwork. The rung beads connect the legs. You can change the look of this edging by changing the number and type of beads used to make the legs and rungs and by changing the gap between the bridges where the thread is attached to the fabric (Mandala Edge Figure A).

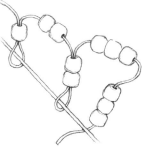

Mandala Edge Figure A

Rolled Edging

Rolled edging serves to completely cover an edge of fabric. It looks something like piping along the edge of a pillow. You need seed beads, beading thread, and a beading needle.

Rolled Edging

This technique is best for the edge of a fabric or beaded surface with a tight weave. Adding a rolled edging to the outermost warp thread of loomwork can crowd the rows, so I don't recommend it.

1. With the thread coming out of the back of the piece along the edge, string seed beads. I find that an odd number of beads looks better because it allows the edging to curve more smoothly. Use just enough beads to span the thickness of the fabric layers, usually 5, 7, or 9 beads.

2. Pass through the layers from the front edge, about a bead's width over from where you last exited the fabric.

3. Repeat all around, crowding the stitches at the corners to make the stitching look fuller. Keep the stitches evenly spaced and close together (Rolled Edge Figure A).

Rolled Edge Figure A

"Hee Haw" Edging

This edging may at first glance seem complicated, but once you understand the rhythm, it is as easy as can be. It gives a very lacy effect. Simply changing the beads used for the "hee" or the "haw" provides an endless variety of looks, so the technique is very versatile. You need seed beads, beading thread, and a beading needle.

1. Anchor your thread in the beadwork. String 5 beads, pass into the edge of the beadwork from front to back, and pass back through the last bead of the 5 just added.

2. * String 13 beads. Pass into the beadwork from front to back about ¼" from the first set of beads and pass back through the last 2 beads of the 13 just added.

3. String 3 beads. Backing up the width of a few beads, pass into the beadwork from front to back and back up through the last bead of the 3 just added (Hee-Haw Edge Figure A).

4. Repeat from * around the edge of the beadwork.

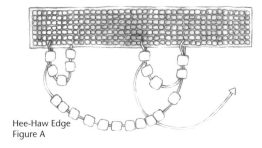

Hee-Haw Edge
Figure A

FRINGES

The secret to great fringe is the tension. Most fringe should be tight enough not to leave a gap, yet loose enough to be soft and flowing. Fringe that is too tight looks stiff and kinked.

Fringe is worked right into beadwork. To begin, pass through either beads or layers of fabric.

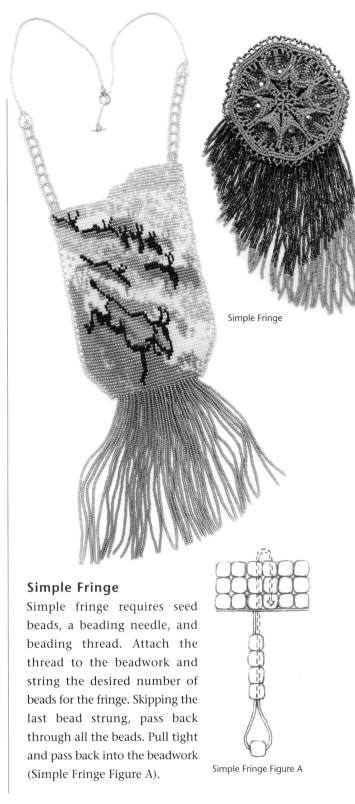

Simple Fringe

Simple Fringe

Simple fringe requires seed beads, a beading needle, and beading thread. Attach the thread to the beadwork and string the desired number of beads for the fringe. Skipping the last bead strung, pass back through all the beads. Pull tight and pass back into the beadwork (Simple Fringe Figure A).

Simple Fringe Figure A

Two-Legged Fringe

For two-legged fringe, you need seed beads, a beading needle, and beading thread. Attach the thread to the beadwork and string the desired number of beads for the fringe.

Skipping the last bead strung pass back through several of the beads just added. Pull tight. String the number of beads that remain at the top of the first leg.

Pull tight. Pass back into the beadwork a short space from the first leg (Two-Legged Fringe Figure A).

Loose Branch or Grass Fringe   Stiff Branch Fringe

Stiff Branch Fringe

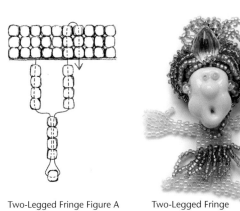

Two-Legged Fringe Figure A   Two-Legged Fringe

Branch Fringe

Branch fringe uses seed beads, beading thread, and a beading needle. String seed beads for the desired length of the fringe. Skipping the last bead strung, pass back through a few beads.

String enough seed beads for a branch, push aside the last bead strung, and pass back through the beads. Add branches randomly, working in the same fashion all the way up the fringe.

To vary the look of the branches, change the tension in the thread, the weight of thread you use, and the way you anchor branches to the main fringe. For a stiff branch fringe, pass back through the bead you

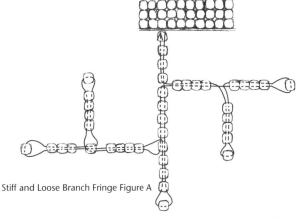

Stiff and Loose Branch Fringe Figure A

exit and keep the tension tight (Stiff and Loose Branch Fringe Figure A). For a looser, more flowing fringe that looks like grass, use less tension and don't pass back through the bead on the main fringe.

Twisted Fringe

For this fringe, you need seed beads, a beading needle, and beading thread. Attach to the beadwork and string twice the number of beads necessary for the length of the fringe you want. You can either measure the fringe or count the number of beads.

Suspend the beadwork by the thread used for

Twisted Fringe

stringing the fringe. Holding the working thread up so it is free from any interference with the fringe beads, pinch the working thread ½" away from the last bead strung for the fringe. If you are right-handed, pinch with the left hand; if left-handed, use the right.

Keep the thread pinched firmly while you spin the beadwork around to twist the thread. As the thread twists, it will slowly reduce the space between the last bead and the fingers used for pinching the thread. When the bead reaches the fingers, you are ready to finish the fringe. Do not let go of the thread, even for a second (Twisted Fringe Figure A).

This next step feels a little awkward at first, but after a few times, you will be comfortable with it. Still holding the thread, lay the beadwork in a position that is comfortable to work with. Pass

Twisted Fringe Figure A

into the edge of the beadwork and carefully pull the thread through until you meet the fingers pinching the thread. Let go and pull the thread the rest of the way. Back it out a bit if the fringe does not twist up.

Hold the piece up and let the fringe relax into position. The tension created when you were twisting will relax somewhat, but the beads will hold in most of the twist. If you wish, tie a half hitch knot between beads of the main body to secure the fringe.

Looped Fringe

For this fringe, you need seed beads, a beading needle, and beading thread. Attach to the beadwork. String enough beads to make as big a loop as you wish. Pass through the edge of the work. Repeat as desired, combining different lengths and types of beads (Looped Fringe Figure A). You can also alter the space between the ends of the loop for different effects.

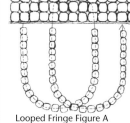

Looped Fringe

Looped Fringe Figure A

Corkscrew Fringe

Corkscrew fringe is based on simple fringe, but this fringe involves square stitch for a corkscrew effect. It requires seed beads, a beading needle, and beading thread.

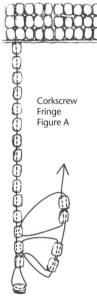

Corkscrew Fringe Figure A

Attach to the beadwork and string enough beads for your desired length of fringe. Skipping the last bead strung, pass back through at least one bead. Leave at least two beads' worth of space between the fringe and the beadwork to accommodate the tension of the next row. Square-stitch 2 beads at a time along the length of the fringe (Corkscrew Fringe Figure A).

The beads will twist around as you work. If the beads get too tight, you can break one of them.

To break a bead safely, you have two options. You can slide a large needle or awl into the bead, bursting it from the inside out, or you can slide a needle into the bead to protect the thread, then pinch the bead with pliers or the corner of fingernail clippers. However, if you use pliers or clippers, you risk breaking the thread. In either case, be sure to close your eyes when you break a bead—sometimes the shards fly up.

You can work the corkscrew sections for only part of the length of the fringe—simply stop square-stitching and pass the needle back through the fringe (Cork-

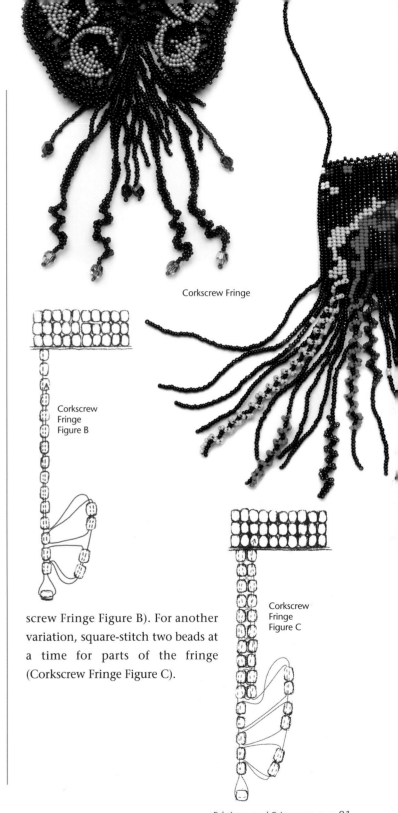

Corkscrew Fringe

Corkscrew Fringe Figure B

Corkscrew Fringe Figure C

screw Fringe Figure B). For another variation, square-stitch two beads at a time for parts of the fringe (Corkscrew Fringe Figure C).

Rooster Tails

This technique works best for fringe less than 3" long. You need seed beads, beading thread, and a beading needle. For peyote stitch instructions, see page 108.

Attach to the beadwork. String an odd number of beads. Skipping the last bead strung, pass back through 2 beads. Work peyote stitch, increasing by stringing 2 beads in the first and third sets. Work the rest of the row using 1 bead for each peyote stitch (Rooster Tail Fringe Figure A).

For thicker fringe, work 2 more rows. Use 2 beads in the sets at the end of the fringe.

To make each rooster tail different, work increases in random order and alter the number of beads for the base.

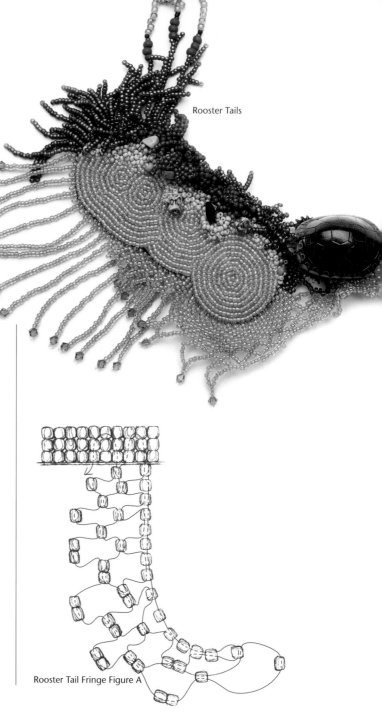

Rooster Tails

Rooster Tails

Rooster Tail Fringe Figure A

Daisy-Tipped Fringe Earrings

A simple fringe can add interest and style to even the smallest of projects. These easy earrings are a good introduction to several seed bead techniques and a good way to practice making fringe.

Materials

¼ tube of cream 11° Japanese seed beads
¼ tube of silver-lined peach 11° Japanese seed beads
10 small cream or peach seed pearls
Six 6mm padparadcha pink Austrian crystals
Six 8mm padparadcha pink Austrian crystals
Beading thread
2 ear wires

Notions

Size 12 beading needle
Scissors

1. For the foundation, work a base of ladder stitch 5 beads across (see Basic stitches, page 108).
2. Work 3 rows of brick stitch, decreasing each row so you end with 2 beads.

3. Now work the spacer and daisy for the loop. String 9 seed beads. Skip the first bead strung and pass through the second and third beads of the 9 just added. Pull the thread tight so the beads form a circle. String a silver-lined bead and pass through the 2 beads (6 and 7) at the top of the circle, opposite beads 2 and 3 (Daisy-Tipped Fringe Earrings Figure A).
4. For the loop, string 7 silver-lined beads. Pass back through all 7, pulling the thread tight so the beads form a circle. Pass through all 7 beads several times to strengthen.
5. Weave through the beads of the daisy and along the edge beads of the brick stitch. Exit from the first bead of the foundation row.
6. String on the beads of the fringe following the chart (Daisy-Tipped Fringe Earrings Figure B).
7. Work a daisy along the end of the fringe. String 8 beads, pass back through the first 2 beads of the 8 for the daisy, string 1 silver-lined bead, and pass back though the last 2 beads.
8. Pass through the body of the fringe and through the first bead of the foundation. Pass back through the second bead of the foundation and begin the second fringe. Work all five fringes across the bottom of the earring base. Weave the thread into the work and tie off in a discreet place.
9. Make a second earring. Add ear wires to each.

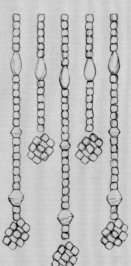

Daisy-Tipped Fringe Earrings Figure A

Daisy-Tipped Fringe Earrings Figure B

ADDING STRAPS TO BEADWORK

In principle, using thread to connect a beaded strap to a beaded centerpiece is the same as making any other kind of necklace or bracelet with any other materials. However, the beadwork in the strap and in the centerpiece has unique dynamics and characteristics to keep in mind. For example, as a necklace is worn, its weight can place stress on the threads and pull them out of shape. The fibers of a backed piece can fray if the weight is not balanced properly.

It's important to consider the strength of the strap and the weight of the centerpiece. If too much weight rests on a single bead in the strap or in the centerpiece, the bead can break.

Weaving threads through several beads or rows of the work disperses the weight so that many beads and fibers of the beaded fabric share the stress. You may want the strap to look as if it exits from a single bead, but weaving the thread into the beadwork helps bear the beads' weight and strengthen the fabric of the thread between the beads.

Attaching some straps requires many strands of fine thread instead of heavy beading cord or wire. That's because the holes in some beads are often too small to accept the cords most often used for straps.

When you're using fine thread, it is a good idea to work the whole strap with a doubled thread. Pass the thread from the clasp through the strap, attach it to the centerpiece, and pass back through to the clasp. After this doubled thread is secured, you can pass a new thread through all the elements. This technique gives you two separate threads that are separately secured. If one wears out, there is a good chance that the second one won't. To disperse the weight even more, you can also use a different thread path at the point of attachment for the two threads.

No matter which stitch you use, you can weave the threads in to accommodate the centerpiece. Simply follow the thread path of each stitch as you weave the threads in.

ATTACHING TO PEYOTE AND BRICK STITCH

To attach a strap using more than one needle, select a bead at the spot where you want to add one end of the strap. Weave through a bead at the edge of the beadwork, leaving a tail long enough to work the strap. Weave down into the beadwork's body for a few rows, then weave back up, exiting through the same edge bead. You will have two threads coming out of the bead in opposite directions. Repeat on other beads across the edge to attach other straps (Adding a Strap to Peyote or Brick Stitch Figure A).

For a single-needle strap, burn or tie a knot on the end of the thread. Pass through a few beads at the edge and tie a knot on the thread between the beads. Work the needle to the point where you want the strap and weave through the beads up to the bead on the edge.

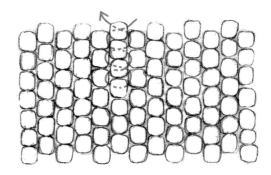

Adding a Strap to Peyote or Brick Stitch Figure A

ATTACHING TO LOOMWORK

For vertical loomwork, or work in which the rows rest vertically when the piece is worn, add the strap along the edge warp thread. You also need to make an extra effort to balance the beadwork properly. This will involve dispersing the weight of the strap over at least two rows (Adding a Strap to Loomwork Figure A).

When you're adding a strap to a loomwork piece in which the rows rest horizontally, it is often best to plan the strap before you do any loomwork, so that you can adjust the number of warp threads. Then you can use the warp threads for the strap—either woven or using an off-loom stitch such as peyote.

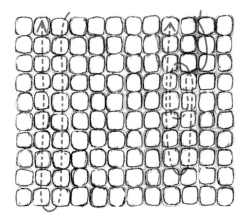

Adding a Strap to Loomwork Figure A

Loomwork with Strap

GALLERY

Margie Deeb
Marietta, Georgia
12" L, 2¼" W

Barbara Grainger
Oregon City, Oregon
10½" L

Jeannette Cook
Lemon Grove, California
Varying sizes

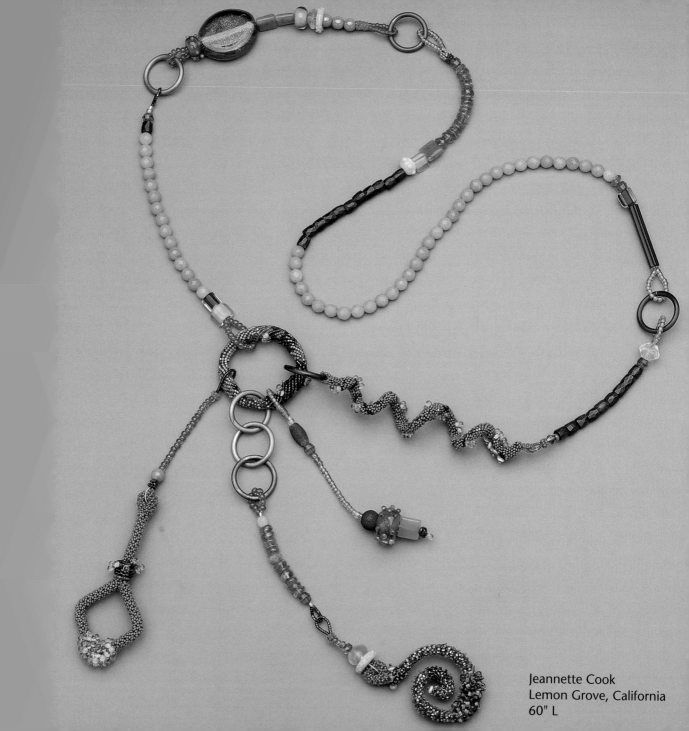

Jeannette Cook
Lemon Grove, California
60" L

Lucy Elle
Seattle, Washington
15" L

Nicole Campanella
Mullan, Idaho
16" L, 1¼" W

Frieda Bates
Carlsbad, New Mexico
18" L, 1¾" W

Frieda Bates
Carlsbad, New Mexico
15" L

Suzanne Golden
New York, New York
6½" L

Suzanne Golden
New York, New York
23" L, center 5" W

Red Ventling
Livingston, Montana
19¼" L, 2⅝" W

Virginia Blakelock
Wilsonville, Oregon
61" L

Jean Campbell
Eden Prairie, Minnesota
6" L

Jean Campbell
Eden Prairie, Minnesota
6½" L

Jan Wasser
Spokane, Washington
13½" L, 3¾" W

Judy Kintner
Spokane, Washington
9½" L, 2" W

Michael Barley
Port Townsend, Washington
12" L ea.

Toni McMahon
Colbert, Washington
11" L

Sharon Bateman
Rathdrum, Idaho
17¼" L, 2⅛" W

BASIC STITCHES

BRICK STITCH

Brick stitch is also known as "Comanche weave." Begin by creating a foundation row in ladder stitch. String one bead and pass through the closest exposed loop of the foundation row. Pass back through the same bead and continue, adding one bead at a time.

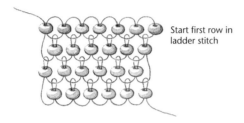

Start first row in ladder stitch

HOOK STITCH

With the hook stitch, you attach a thread to the edge of beadwork so you can work an edging. When adding edgings to loomwork, run the hook thread under the warp thread along the outer edge. When adding edging to an embroidered piece or a cabochon, pass the hook through all layers of fabric. When working an edge along a piece of off-loom beadwork, pass the hook through each individual bead.

To hook stitch over an earring wire, pass through a bead, over the wire, and pass down through the same bead.

LADDER STITCH

Using two needles, one threaded on each end of the thread, pass one needle through one or more beads from left to right and pass the other needle through the same beads from right to left. Continue adding beads by criss-cross-

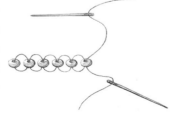

ing both needles through one bead at a time. Use this stitch to make strings of beads or as the foundation for brick stitch.

PEYOTE STITCH

This stitch is often called gourd stitch.

Even-count flat peyote stitch

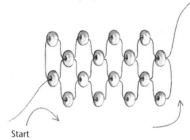

Start

Begin by stringing an even number of beads, twice the number you want in one row. These beads will become the first and second rows. Create the next row by stringing one bead and passing through the second-to-last bead of the previous row. String another bead and pass through the fourth-to-last bead of the previous row. Continue adding one bead at a time, passing over every other bead of the previous row.

Odd-count flat peyote stitch

Begin by stringing an odd number of beads (our example shows five). These beads will become the first and second rows. Begin the next row by adding a bead and passing through the second-to-last bead just strung, bead four in our example. Continue as with even-count peyote. When you reach the end of the row, pass through beads one, two, and three. Pass through the second-to-last bead in what has now become the third row. Pass back through beads two and one (in that order). Pass through the last bead

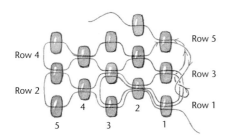

Row 5
Row 4
Row 3
Row 2
Row 1
5   4   3   2   1

added in Row 3. Continue across Row 4 in regular peyote. Start Row 5 as you began Row 3. At the end of Row 5, exit from the last bead added and loop thread through the outer edge threads (not beads) of the previous row. Pass back through the last bead added and continue across the row adding one bead at a time.

Tubular peyote stitch

Begin by determining the diameter of the form you wish to cover. Thread an even number of beads to fit in a circle over this form. Make a circle by passing through all the strung beads twice more, exiting from the first bead strung. String one bead and pass through the third bead of the first round. String one bead and pass through the fifth bead of the first round. Continue adding one bead at a time, skipping over one bead of the first round, until you have added half the number of beads of the first round. Exit from the first bead of the second

round. Slide the work onto the form. String one bead, pass through the second bead added in the second round and pull thread tight. String one bead and pass through the third bead added in the second round. Continue around, filling in the "spaces," one bead at a time. Exit from the first bead added in each round.

Peyote stitch decrease

To make a row-end decrease, simply stop your row short and begin a new row.

To make a hidden row-end decrease, pass through the last bead on a row. Weave your thread between two beads of the previous row, looping it around the thread that connects the beads. Pass

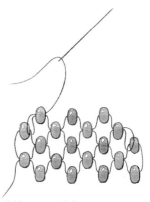

Hidden row-end decrease

back through the last bead of the row just worked and continue across in regular flat peyote.

To make a mid-project decrease, simply pass thread through two beads without adding a bead in the "gap." In the next row, work a regular one-drop peyote over the decrease. Keep tension taut to avoid holes.

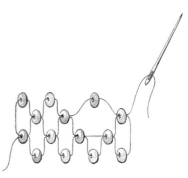

Mid-project decrease

Peyote stitch increase

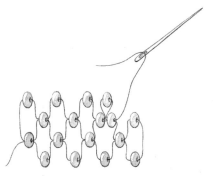

Make a mid-project increase by working a two-drop over a one-drop in one row. In the next row work a one-drop peyote between the two-drop. For a smooth increase, use very narrow beads for both the two-drop and the one-drop between.

PICOT EDGING

Picot edging creates a playful frame of little points around a finished piece and works really well for sewing two pieces of fabric together at the edge. To practice the picot edge stitch, make a fold in your fabric. Secure your thread on the underside of the fold and come through the fold to the surface of the fabric. String three beads, and *at about the distance of one bead from where you started, sew across the folded edge of your fabric from the back to the front. Without piercing the fabric again, go up through the last bead strung and string on two more beads. Repeat from the *.

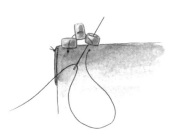

• To create a taller picot edge, start by stringing five beads and go up through the last two. Then from that point, string three at a time. Space the stitches about the width of one bead.
• Experiment using different sizes and colors of beads. Try using a larger bead or a different color for the point.

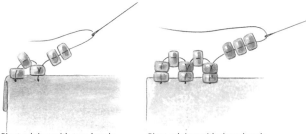

Picot edging with two beads   Picot edging with three beads

SINGLE CROCHET WITH BEADS

To work a bead in single crochet, insert the hook into the back of the stitch, put the yarn over the hook and draw a loop through— you now have two loops on the hook.

Slide a bead up to the loops, wrap yarn over the hook, and draw the yarn through the loops. The bead will be fixed to the back side of the crocheted work.

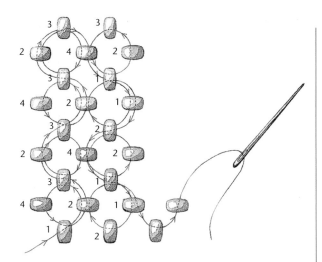

SINGLE-NEEDLE RIGHT-ANGLE WEAVE

The illustration refers to bead positions—these are not bead numbers, but position numbers.

Row 1: String four base beads. Pass through beads in positions 1, 2, and 3. The bead in position 3 will become the bead in position 1 in the next group. String three beads. Pass through bead in position 3 of last group (now position 1 of this group), bead in position 2 and bead in position 3 (now position 1 of next group). String three beads. Continue working in this pattern until the row is to a desired length. In the last group, pass through beads in positions 1, 2, 3, and 4.

Row 2: String three beads. Pass through bead in position 4 of previous group and bead in position 1 of this group. String two beads. Pass through bead in position 2 of Row 1, bead in position 1 of previous group, and the beads just added. Pass through bead in position 4 of Row 1. String two beads. Pass through bead in position 2 of previous group and bead in position 4 of Row 1. Pass through first bead just added. String two beads. Pass through bead in position 2 of Row 1, bead in position 1 of previous group, and the first bead just added.

Row 3: Repeat Row 2.

SQUARE STITCH

Begin by stringing a row of beads. For the second row, string two beads, pass through the second-to-last bead of the first row, and back through the second bead of those just strung. Continue by stringing one bead, passing through the third-to-last bead of the first row, and back through the bead just strung. Repeat this looping technique across to the end of the row.

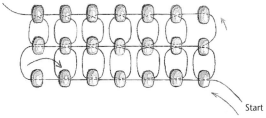

STOPPER (TENSION) BEAD

A tension bead (or stopper bead) holds your work in place. To make one, string a bead larger than those you are working with, then pass through the bead twice, making sure not to split your thread. The bead will be able to slide, but will still provide tension to work against when you're beading the first two rows.

WIRE SPIRAL

To start a spiral, make a small loop at the end of a wire with round-nose pliers. Enlarge the piece by holding on to the spiral with chain-nose pliers and pushing the wire over the previous coil with your thumb.

SUPPLIERS & RESOURCES

SUPPLIERS

A Beaucoup Conge
www.beadholiday.com
(520) 696-9490
355 E. Lowell
Tucson, AZ 85705-3924
   Beads, Beadalon wires and cords, basic beading supplies, tools, Swarovski crystal, vintage pressed glass

Art from Greece
www.artfromgreece.com/index.html
(941) 330-1621
4411 Bee Ridge Rd., #125
Sarasota, FL 34233
   Replicas of ancient clasps

ArtBeads.com
www.artbeads.com
(866) 715-BEAD (2323)
NW Corporate Park, Ste. 145
7901 Skansie Ave.
Gig Harbor, WA 98335
   Silver findings, beads, spacers

Ayla's Originals
www.aylasoriginals.com
(847) 328-4040
1511 Sherman Ave.
Evanston, IL 60201
   Glass beads, dichroic glass, silver, Swarovski crystal, freshwater pearls

Beadalon
www.beadalon.com
(866) 423-2325
205 Carter Dr.
West Chester, PA 19382
   Stringing wire, elastic bead cord, memory wire, findings

BeadBabe.com
www.beadbabe.com
(800) 270-4181
5710 Auburn Blvd., #3
Sacramento, CA 95841
   Specialty beads, natural beads, stringing wire, tools

Beadcats/Universal Synergetics

www.beadcats.com

PO Box 2840

Wilsonville, OR 97070-2840

   Beads, books, basic supplies

Burkett Studio

(505) 722-7077

601 S. Second St.

Gallup, NM 87301

   Specialty beads, clasps

Carl Clasmeyer

www.clasmeyer.com

(505) 989-5711

Clasmeyer Studios

PO Box 31911

Santa Fe, NM 87594

   Specialty beads, connectors, clasps

Cindy's Crafts

members.tripod.com/~cindycrafts/\
beadlady.htm

Phone/Fax (423) 926-0050

2532 Elizabethton Hwy.

Johnson City, TN 37601

   Beading supplies and books

Fire Mountain Gems

www.firemountaingems.com

(800) 355-2137

1 Fire Mountain Wy.

Grants Pass, OR 97526-2373

   Seed beads, glass beads, metal beads, findings

Green Girl Studios

www.greengirlstudios.com

(213) 365-9806

711 S. Rampart Blvd., #301

Los Angeles, CA 90057

   Specialty beads, silver and pewter findings

Jess Imports

www.jessimports.com/catalog.html

(510) 839-4793

366 Grand Ave., #271

Oakland, CA 94610

   Specialty clasps

Mill Hill

www.millhill.com

(608) 754-9466

PO Box 1060

Janesville, WI 53547-1060

   Magnifica beads, seed beads, lead crystal, decorative beads

Red Horse Ranch

www.redhorseranch.com

(949) 509-9512

25602 Alicia Pkwy., PMB 206

Laguna Hills, CA 92653

  Carved Tagua nut focal beads

Rings and Things

www.rings-things.com

(800) 366-2156

214 N. Wall St., Ste. 990

PO Box 450

Spokane, WA 99210-0450

  Beads, findings, basic beading and wire working supplies

Rio Grande

www.riogrande.com

(800) 545-6566

7500 Bluewater Rd. NW

Albuquerque, NM 87121

  Findings, beads, stringing material

Rishashay

www.rishashay.com

(800) 517-3311

PO Box 8271

Missoula, MT 59807

  Sterling silver beads, clasps, connectors

Scottsdale Bead Supply

www.scottsdalebead.com

(480) 945-5988

3625 N. Marshall Wy.

Scottsdale, AZ 85251

  Clasps, toggles

Shipwreck Beads

www.shipwreckbeads.com

(800) 950-4232

8560 Commerce Pl. Dr. NE

Lacey, WA 98516

  Seed beads, glass beads, metal beads, tools

Soft Flex

www.SoftFlexCompany.com

(707) 938-3539

PO Box 80

Sonoma, CA 95476

  Artistic wire, findings, glass beads

Sojourner

www.sojourner.biz

(609) 397-8849

26 Bridge St.

Lambertville, NJ 08530

  Freshwater pearls, specialty beads, clasps, Swarovski crystals

Somerset-silver.com
Cheron Gelber
4537140th Ave. S.E.
Bellevue, WA 98006
Thai silver beads and findings

Thunderbird Supply Co.
www.thunderbirdsupply.com
(800) 545-7968
1907 West Hwy. 66
Gallup, NM 87301 or
2311 Vassar
Albuquerque, NM 87107-1827
Precious and base metals, findings, tools, stones, strands, shells

RESOURCES

Books

Mascetti, Daniela, and Amanda Triossi. *Earrings: From Antiquity to the Present.* New York: Thames and Hudson, 1999.

_____. *The Necklace: From Antiquity to the Present.* New York: Harry N. Abrams, 1997.

Web Resources
History: General
Greek Jewelry—Five Thousand Years of Tradition,http://www.addgr.com/jewel/elka/index.html

History of Western Philosophy-Summary Outline by Patrick Distante, http://home.earthlink.net/~pdistan/

Odysseus, the WWW server of the Hellenic Ministry of Culture, http://www.culture.gr/home /welcome.html

Washington State University, World Civilization http://www.wsu.edu:8080/~dee/world.htm

History of Materials and Metals
Copper, http://www.copper.org/

Glass, http://cornucopia-of-colors.com/history. html, and http://www.glassonline.com/history. html

Gold, http://www.gold.org/index.html

Needles, http://www.entaco.com/intro.htm

Pearls, http://www.pbs.org/wgbh/nova/pearl/freshwater.html

Silver, http://www.silverinstitute.org

Swarovski Crystals, http://www.signity.com/company/swarovski.htm and http://www.mortonscrytal.com/page23.htm

INDEX

A

adding straps 84
adding threads 73
anchoring 72, 73

B

Babylonians 3
backed beadwork 32
    findings with 74, 75
bails 31–33, 34
Bali spacers 43
barrel clasp 51
bars, spacing 27
basic earrings 25
bayonet clasp 47, 48
bead caps 28–30
bead tips 37
beaded loop clasp 59
bead-stacked pins 27
beads 8–10, 11
    bugle 9
    chips 9
    cylinder 8, 9
    carnelian 3
    crystals 10
    Czech 8
    Delica 8
    druks 9
    faceted 9, 10
    glass 10, 11
    Japanese 8
    lampworked 10
    Magnifica 8
natural 3, 9
    Neolithic 3
    nuggets 9
    pearls 9
    seed 8, 9
    stone 9
    Toho 8
bending wire 18
blocks 14, 15
bolo terminal 36

box clasp 49
branch fringe 79
brick stitch 108
    attaching straps to 84
    ending thread 73
Brick-Stitched Flower Pin 68
Bronze Age 3–4
buckle clasp 52
bugle beads 9
bullion 46
Button Connector Earrings 21

C

caps, bead 28, 29, 30, 42–43
carnelian beads 3
chips 9
clamshell tips 37
clasps 32, 46–63
    barrel 51
    bayonet 47, 48
    beaded loop 59
    box 5, 49
    buckle 52
    designer 52
    fishhook 47
    fishhook crimp 47
    fishhook with spring catch 47
    fold-over 48
    jigged wire 54
    lanyard 52
    lariat 51
    lobster claw 49
    macaroni toggle 55
    manufactured 46
    overlapping 75, 76
    pearl 50
    "S" hook 48
    sister hook 48
    slide 51
    sling 58
    spring ring 50
    square-stitched toggle 56
    to make 52

toggle 50, 55–56, 57
torpedo 51
two-hole bead 53, 54
vintage 5
clutch pins 69
connectors 27, 30, 31, 34
corkscrew fringe 81
cord 12
crimp
    hoops 64
    safety 45
    tubes 45
crimping 14
    how to 44
crimps 44–45, 46
    with attached jump ring 45, 46
crochet ropes and jump ring terminals 42
crochet, single with beads 110
crystals 10
cup burr 14
cutting wire 18
cylinder beads 8, 9
Czech beads 8

D

daisy spacers 43
Daisy-Tipped Fringe Earrings 83
Delica beads 8
designer clasps 52
donut toggle 55, 56
druks 9

E

ear wires 64–67, 68
earrings 25, 26, 27
edgings 76–77, 110
    hee haw 78
    mandala 77
    rolled 77
Egyptians 4
Eyeglass Terminals 41
Embellished Wire Hoops 65–66

ending threads 73, 74
eye pins 24

F
faceted beads 9, 10
findings 24–69
finishings 71–85
fishhook clasp 47
fishhook clasp with spring catch 47
fishhook crimp clasp 47
fold-over clasp 48
    multiple-strand 49
fold-over terminal 35
fringes 76, 79–83
    branch 79
    corkscrew 81
    looped 80
    rooster tails 82
    simple 78
    twisted 80
    two-legged 79

G
gallery artists 88–106
    Barley, Michael 104
    Bateman, Sharon 106
    Bates, Frieda 94, 95
    Blakelock, Virginia 99
    Campanella, Nicole 93
    Campbell, Jean 100, 101
    Cook, Jeannette 90, 91
    Deeb, Margie 88
    Elle, Lucy 92
    Golden, Suzanne 96, 97
    Grainger, Barbara 89
    Kintner, Judy 103
    McMahon, Toni 105
    Ventling, Red 98
    Wasser, Jan 102
glass beads 10, 11
glued bullet ends 36

H
half hitch knot 72
hammer 15
hat pins 69
head pin ear wires 27
head pins 24–25
hee haw edging 78
hook stitch 108
hook-stitched hoops 65

J
Japanese beads 8
jig 19, 20
Jigged Ear Wires 67
jigged wire clasp 54
jump rings 20, 30
    crimps with attached jump ring 45, 46
    making 30
    terminals 42

K
kidney wires 64
knots 72, 73
    cord 28
    half hitch 72
    lark's head 72
    love 41
    overhand, multiple 72
knotted cord spacing 28

L
ladder stitch 108
lampworked beads 10
lanyard clasp 52
lariat clasp 51
lariat necklace with self-clasp 57
lark's head knot 72
links 20–21
lobster claw clasp 49
loomwork 12
    adding and ending threads 73
    attaching straps to 85

looped fringe 80
loops, making 18
    terminal 44
Love Knots 41

M
macaroni toggle 55
Magnifica beads 8
Making a Wire Bail 34
mandala edging 77
materials 8–12, 13
measuring wire 18
Monkey's Fist Pendant Bail 33

N
natural beads 3, 9
needles 13
Neolithic 3
netting
    adding and ending thread 74
    seed bead terminal 40
Nymo 12
nuggets 9

O
Omega Terminal 38, 39
overhand knots, multiple 72
overlapping clasp 75, 76

P
pearl clasp 50
pearls 9
Peyote Bracelet with Bent Wire Created Clasp 63
peyote stitch
    adding and ending thread 74
    attaching straps to 84
    bracelet with macaroni/donut toggle clasp 55
    decrease 109
    flat 108, 109
    increase 110
    seed bead terminal 39, 40

tubular 109
peyote-stitched bracelet with macaroni/donut toggle clasp 55–56, 57
peyote-stitched seed bead cap 29, 30
picot edging 110
pin points, making 18
pins 69
pliers 13, 14
Pomegranate Stitch Bracelet with Geometric Clasp 60–62

R
reamers 14
resources 113
right-angle weave
    ending thread 74
    single needle 110, 111
rolled edging 77
rooster tails fringe 82

S
"S" hook clasp 48
safety crimp 46
safety-type pins 69
seed bead
    cap 28, 29, 30
    spirals 27
    terminals 38–40
    terminals with netting 40
    terminals with peyote stitch 39, 40
    tubes 30
seed beads 8, 9
    cylinder 8
    Czech 8
    Japanese 8
Silamide 12
simple fringe 78
single crochet with beads 110
single-needle right-angle weave 110, 111

sister hook clasp 48
slide clasp 51
Sling Clasp Bracelet 58
smoothers 14
spacer terminal 38
spacers 43
spacing
    bars and connectors 27–28
    knotted cord 28
spring ring clasp 50
spring terminal 34
square stitch 111
    ending and adding thread 74
square-stitched
    beaded bail 31
    seed bead cap 29
    toggle clasp 56, 57
Squiggle Pins 26
staple bend pins 24
starter stick 15
sterling silver tubes 45
stitches 108–111
Stone Age 3
stone beads 9
stopper bead 111
straightening wire 18
straps, adding 84–85
Sumerians 3
suppliers 112, 113

T
tails, thread 73
Teddy Bear Terminal 39
tempering wire 18, 19
terminals 34–42, 44
    bead tips 37
    bolo 36
    clamshells 37
    eyeglass 41
    fold-over 35
    glued bullet ends 36
    jump ring, with crocheted ropes 42

loops 44
manufactured 34
Omega 38
seed bead 38–40
spacer 38
spring 34
Teddy Bear 39
two-hole 38
wired bullet ends 35, 36
threads 11–12, 13
    adding and ending 73, 74
toggle clasps 50
Toho beads 8
tools 13–15
torpedo clasp 51
tubes
    crimp 45
    seed bead 30
    sterling silver 45
20 Picots Hoop 66
20 Picots Rainbow Ruffle Hoops 66
twisted fringe 80
two-hole bead clasp 53, 54
Two-Hole Bead Spirals 68
two-hole terminal 38
two-legged fringe 79

W
wire bails 32–33, 34
wire spiral 111
wires 11–12, 13
bullet end 35, 36
hoops, embellished 64, 65, 66
wires
    crimp hoops, using 64
    ear 64–67
    kidney wires, 64
    manufactured 64
    wire hoops, using 64
wireworking 17–21, 63